THE OLD SALEM

TOY MUSEUM

Thomas A. Gray

Boy with a Drum

During the mid-eighteenth century, portraits often depicted their subjects with symbolic toys, as shown in Boy with a Drum, ca. 1760-70. A leading painter in the New England area, Joseph Blackburn (ca. 1700-83), signed this delightful oil-on-canvas portrait upon its completion in either Boston, Massachusetts, or London, England.

Anne P. and Thomas A. Gray Purchase Fund—5122, in honor of Barbara Babcock Millhouse

THE OLD SALEM

TOY MUSEUM

Thomas A. Gray

Old Salem Inc.
The Old Salem Toy Museum
Winston-Salem, North Carolina

Cover images: Tinplate merry-go-round by Märklin, ca. 1905, Germany (also illustrated in figure 3.2). The cover background is taken from the box top of Albert Schoenhut's "Humpty-Dumpty Circus," 1903, Philadelphia (illustrated in figure 3.4b).

© 2005 Old Salem Inc.
Edited by Gary J. Albert
Photography by Wes Stewart
Design and Typography by Claire Purnell, Annapolis, MD

Printed in the USA by Jostens, Winston-Salem, NC

This book was typeset in Bodoni and Avenir typefaces and
printed on 80-pound Centura dull text stock and Carolina C1S cover stock.

LIBRARY OF CONGRESS CATALOGING-IN-PUBLICATION DATA

Old Salem Toy Museum.
    The Old Salem Toy Museum / by Thomas A. Gray.— 1st ed.
        p. cm. — (The Old Salem Toy Museum series)
    Includes bibliographical references.
    ISBN 1-879704-09-9
    1. Toys—Catalogs. 2. Toys—North Carolina—Winston-Salem—Catalogs. 3. Old Salem Toy Museum—Catalogs. I. Gray,
Thomas A. II. Title. III. Series.
NK9509.4.W560436 2005
745.592'074'75667—dc22

                                                                                                                    2005010778

TABLE OF CONTENTS

FOREWORD

THE simple word "toy" makes anyone smile because it awakens memories. The word also produces nostalgia for childhood. Toys were intended for amusement and education, and they delighted their small owners and aided them in their discovery of the world around them. If a toy has not been "loved to death" during childhood it is usually easy to cherish into adulthood due to its small size and because of the heart's attachment to it.

Like children around the world, those who lived in one of the historic Moravian towns in piedmont North Carolina – Bethabara, Bethania, Salem, Friedberg, Freidland, or Hope – played with toys, and, because of this, toys have been part of the extensive Old Salem collection since the museum began in 1950. Most of Old Salem's toys date from the nineteenth century, and we are fortunate in many cases to know who owned and played with these charming treasures. Many of them were imported from Germany, the toy-making capital of the world at that time, but some were made in Moravian homes or by one of the talented local craftsmen. It is important to remember that the toys enjoyed by Moravian children were just a part of a much broader universe of toys with histories dating back centuries.

It is this larger historical context of toys that the founders of Old Salem's Toy Museum, Thomas A. Gray and his mother, Anne Pepper Gray, wanted to clearly represent. Tom and Anne have been generous and dedicated supporters of Old Salem for many years. As consummate collectors themselves, they knew that a world-class toy collection could be assembled and that it would have a wide appeal.

After only a few years of intense and purposeful collecting, Tom and Anne had amassed a superb and delightful collection of toys that, along with Old Salem's toy collection, became the Old Salem Toy Museum, located on South Main Street in the Frank L. Horton Museum Center in Winston-Salem, North Carolina. There are toys from Germany, Great Britain, Holland, France, Spain, and America. The oldest toys are metal archaeological finds from the third century dredged from the Thames River in London. The most recent are early-twentieth-century airplanes and automobiles. In-between is a feast for the imagination, and under Tom's careful guidance the collection continues to grow.

With this book Old Salem is pleased to inaugurate a series that will focus on different aspects of the Toy Museum collection. This first volume is intended to provide a colorful survey and a

Anne and Tom Gray at the gala opening of the Old Salem Toy Museum, November 16, 2002. Photograph by David Rosen.

reminder of some of the enchanting highlights found in this amazing and unrivalled collection, and we were delighted when Tom Gray agreed to write it. What better author could there be than one of the founders whose vision, along with his mother's, became a reality in this museum? We are grateful that both Tom and Anne were here for the gala opening of the museum in November 2002 and that they could experience the excitement over the museum and receive the gratitude bestowed on them. Sadly, Anne passed away in July 2003, but her legacy lives on in her many contributions to Old Salem and particularly in the Toy Museum. At this time we again offer our most sincere thanks to Tom and Anne Gray for the outstanding toy museum that they donated to Old Salem. It is a museum with universal appeal that engages our intellect and more importantly speaks to our hearts.

Paula Locklair
Vice President
Museum of Early Southern Decorative Arts
and the Horton Center Museums

FIGURE I.1: THE OLD SALEM TOY MUSEUM

Opened in November 2002, the Toy Museum is located in the Frank L. Horton Museum Center, and through its self-guided tours on two floors, offers a unique, seventeen-hundred-year survey of American, British, and European toys. An extensive library, rare book room, and research facilities on antique toys and social history of children is adjacent to the museum, completing this Old Salem Inc. facility.

INTRODUCTION

FOR my mother and me, putting together the collection of the Old Salem Toy Museum was both a challenge and a joy. Our challenge arose from a desire to broadly survey the full range of toys available to generations of European, British, and American children. Our joy would come from forming a new collection. Having been closely associated with the restoration of Old Salem, and having helped collect the objects needed in the museum's buildings, collecting was in our blood.

Our approach to toys would be unique: a true survey of toys. The few public and private collections of toys concentrate on specific areas, obviously reflecting the chosen interests of the collectors. If we hoped to paint a picture with our toy collection, it was to be with the broadest brushstrokes available.

Old Salem Inc. already exhibited a fine collection of toys once owned by Moravian children in Piedmont, North Carolina. This extraordinary survival of wooden Germanic toys was loved and preserved by the Moravians of Salem. My mother and I wished to place Old Salem's core toy collection in context by surrounding it with a wide scope of European, British, and American toys. In this context, we hoped visitors would more fully appreciate the tastes and interests of children and adults in early-nineteenth-century Salem.

Inspiration to establish the Old Salem Toy Museum originated from two sources. The first was my mentor and cousin Frank L. Horton (1918-2004), who, with his mother, Theo L. Taliaferro (1891-1971), founded the Museum of Early Southern Decorative Arts (MESDA), which opened in Old Salem in 1965. In every aspect of collecting and scholarship, Frank influenced my career. I cannot remember a moment in my life when I didn't stand in the long shadow of this remarkable man. Frank taught my mother and me not to be afraid of founding a museum.

A second, and more specific, source of inspiration must rest with a European trip during the Fall of 1998 that I enjoyed with the founders of the Toy and Miniature Museum of Kansas City, Missouri. Mary Harris Francis, Barbara Hall Marshall, and I toured every major toy museum in Switzerland and Germany, and my eyes were opened to new possibilities at home. Early in the trip I quietly murmured, "Anyone crazy enough to found a toy museum, deserves to go broke...". I soon learned the bitter taste of eating my own words. Returning home, I convinced my mother that a gift

**FIGURES I.2a AND I.2b:
BRASS ADVERTISING
TOKEN (front and reverse)**

*The brass advertising token is a
rare survival of an eighteenth-
century toymaker advertising his
wares. Issued ca. 1760 by John Kirk, a
shopkeeper and engraver from St. Paul's
Churchyard in London, the brass coin depicts
the rich interior of a toy shop, complete with an
attendant waiting on a female customer accompanied by her two young children. On the
reverse, Kirk described the "English and Dutch toys" available. Other tokens by Kirk are in
the collection of the British Museum in London.*

Anne P. and Thomas A. Gray Purchase Fund–4915.1

of the toy museum was not only possible, but also a gift that would grow throughout our lifetimes.

During the relatively short period between that museum trip and the opening of the Old Salem Toy Museum in November 2002, my mother and I voraciously collected the toys needed for the new installation. The seemingly insurmountable task could never have been completed without a core of distinguished "scholar-dealers" literally holding our hands. I have always held that one is only as effective as his closest advisors. Our great friend Anne B. Timpson of Essex Fells, New Jersey, stands on a pedestal above all others—and is, to many, the toy dealer equivalent of the pre-eminent American antiques dealer, the late Israel Sack. Literally, no area of the museum wasn't touched by her deft hands.

Anne's special interest, Victorian-period dollhouses, was enhanced by input from Carolyn Sunstein of Villanova, Pennsylvania, and the superb restoration services of Jeff Fuglestad, Martin O'Brien, Bradshaw and Whelan, and Chuck Baker. The core of our Schoenhut circus collection, originating from the estate of Rosemary Timpson, was completed by my friend Andy Yaffee of Ramsey, New Jersey. Andy has personally directed

FIGURE I.3: TOY SHOP TRADE CARD

Issued a hundred years after the brass advertising token in figures I.2a and b, this engraved trade card was printed ca. 1860 by the toy shop of J.B. Peeters Chopin of Bruges, Belgium. Like the brass token, the interior of this nineteenth-century toy shop is meticulously recorded, with wooden toys likely from the Sonneberg and Erzgebirge areas of Germany arranged in bookcases on the right of the shop.

Anne P. and Thomas A. Gray Purchase Fund–5096

important archival material of the Schoenhut Collectors Club to our museum.

If Anne Timpson served as the principal advisor for the Toy Museum, then another friend, Richard D. Pardue of Winston-Salem, North Carolina, should receive full credit for our unique collection of children's ceramics, proudly the most important of its type outside London. Rick's enthusiastic direction of this collection was offered voluntarily, and we will be eternally in his debt for leading us to Pamela Klaber Roditti, Leo Kaplan, Peter Warren, Simon Spero, Garry Atkins, Jonathan Horne, Felicity Marno, and David Overall, as well as Dragesco-Cramoisan in Paris. Happily, Rick Pardue will author the second title in the Old Salem Toy Museum series, centered on early children's pottery and porcelain, with exceptional new scholarship.

In the area of German wooden toys—one of the Toy Museum's strongest and most important collections—Mary Audrey Apple of Marietta, Georgia, provided critical scholarship, as well as a gift of her personal research materials to our library. Two additional friends, Roy and Grace Olsen of Wayne, Pennsylvania, developed our Germanic collection with, what I believe to be, world-class results.

The earliest toys in the museum, as well as the scholarship necessary to write this book, could never have been acquired without major efforts from Mark and Marjorie Allen of Amherst, New Hampshire, as well as Tom and Jane Campbell of Hawleyville, Connecticut. Friends far before the Toy Museum was conceived, these two couples scoured the English and Dutch countrysides and auction houses for early delft-wares and metalwares. The staff of Christie's in London and New York were essential, too, when we obtained the 1740 baby house from the Vivien Greene Collection, conserved by David Goist of Raleigh, North Carolina, and the George Washington-Nelly Custis paint box, professionally restored by Ned H. Hipp of Bethania, North Carolina. Credit must be given to Katherine Johnson, a 2004 MESDA Summer Institute graduate under Sally W. Gant, director of MESDA education programs, for her research into Washington's multiple purchases of paint boxes for his step-grandchildren.

A new area of the collection, miniature doll-scale furniture, owes its existence to the sharp eyes of friends Alastair and Rosemary Leslie of Perthshire, Scotland, as well as scholarly advice from my friends Robert F. Trent, of Wilmington, Delaware, and John Cross, of London. I am especially indebted to Bob Trent, both for his upholstery skills and the pertinent research to create the caption for the two doll-size "great chairs" (fig. 4.4).

Others who were essential in the formulation of the collection certainly include John Kanuit of Palos Verdes Estates, California, in children's vintage sports equipment; Elizabeth Baird of Portland, Maine, in Christmas and St. Valentine's Day greeting cards; Jim Yeager of Kansas City, Missouri, in American cast-iron toys; and Jo Ann Reisler of Vienna, Virginia, and Helen Younger of Valley Cottage, New York, in juvenile, German-inspired books.

The Old Salem staff, ably led of Paula W. Locklair, vice president of MESDA and the Horton Center museums, expertly directed the Toy Museum installation and was assisted by Johanna Brown, director of collections and curator; Abigail Linville, collections manager; Margaret Shearin, exhibit designer and fabricator; and Katie Schlee, librarian/curator of research collections.

Ann Hall R. Wauford, the initial registrar for the Toy Museum collection, provided the mental muscle and personal enthusiasm critical to opening the new facility. I am indebted to Ann Hall for her additions to this catalog, particularly the discussion of marbles in Chapter 4.

Staples & Charles of Alexandria, Virginia, led by Robert Staples and Barbara Charles, offered the sophisticated designs so needed for the layout of this very diverse collection. The standard phrase we repeated over and over during the museum's design process was that Barbara and Bob were "putting lipstick on the pig"!

If the scholar-dealers and the Old Salem Inc. curatorial staff provided the research both to establish the collection and adequately describe it in this book, then the Old Salem publication staff brought our effort here to fruition. Gary J. Albert, director of publications, provided a superb, professional finish to this neophyte's writing, long rusty from my graduate days in the Winterthur Program. This survey catalog is also the product of the tireless Jennifer Bean Bower, manager of photographic resources; the discerning eye of Wes Stewart, Old Salem's photographer; typing assistance from Paula Chamblee, coordinator of membership services; and design services ably provided by Claire Purnell.

My profound personal thanks to each of these individuals is only surpassed by my appreciation of my mother, Anne P. Gray, who devoted her life to the restoration of Old Salem, embraced the founding of the Toy Museum with her usual enthusiasm, and quietly left us all a celebrated legacy with this gift. Ma, from all of us, the museum and this first catalog can only be dedicated to you.

Thomas A. Gray
July 26, 2004

CHAPTER 1

EARLY TOYS

THE Old Salem Toy Museum presents a fascinating seventeen-hundred-year survey of toys, circa 225 A.D. to 1925. Toys are a window through which we, today, can understand what it was like to be alive at any given moment in time.

Toys are the first objects to which children are exposed and are valuable artifacts that represent the training tools chosen by a society. Studying toys as artifacts, in turn, reflects the social mores and economic atmosphere of specific periods in history. Toys are also evidence of the raw materials available to a culture and of the level of craftsmanship demanded of the artisans of that culture.

By researching and collecting the toys of our ancestors, the Old Salem Toy Museum provides an intriguing pathway to understanding the commercial and intellectual attitudes of a given time and place. Perhaps most importantly, the Toy Museum is shedding new light onto the ways the perception of childhood has evolved over several centuries by studying the objects there were given to children, not just for entertainment, but also to prepare them for adulthood.

The third century in Europe was hardly a time for long life expectancy in children, nor a period of extensive troves of available toys. For four hundred years after its conquest in 43 A.D. by Roman legions under Emperor Claudius, "Londinium" on the Thames River became the trading and capital city of the Roman province of Britannia. Bronze, silver, and lead toys (fig. 1.3), later excavated by mudlarks from numerous dredgings of the Thames, offer a limited glimpse of toys from this early period.

With the approach of the fourteenth century, we have a somewhat clearer picture of toys enjoyed by European children from engravings and manuscripts. The filigreed lead rattle in fig. 1.1 provides an excavated example of metal objects that survive. Wooden hoops, rag dolls, spinning tops, and hand puppets—by the nature of their materials and uses—were more perishable and disposable than metal objects, and thus were more susceptible to destruction during these turbulent years, fraught with plagues and massive fires.

From the late-sixteenth century, the collection of Elizabethan brass firearms (fig. 1.3) in the museum might represent a young Briton's military toys, fashioned after the standard adult muskets and pistols of a time when the Roanoke Island expedition settled the American continent. The fact that some firearms have been unearthed with their barrels blown open attests to the firing qualities

1

of these Elizabethan guns, often overloaded with gunpowder by their over-enthusiastic young owners.

During this time, the Czech Moravian bishop John Amos Comenius (1592-1670), now known as the "father of modern education," was one of the first to advocate a diverse education for boys and girls. His book, *The School of Infancy*, first published in 1633, offered:

Infants try to imitate what they see others do … let them have toys. Leaden knives, wooden swords, ploughs, little carriages, sledges, mills, buildings. With these they may always amuse themselves and thus exercise their bodies to health, their minds to vigor, their bodily members to agility … .

With extensive trading, more prosperous economies, the emergence of a large toy-making trade, and the recognition of the child as a key member of society, children's amusements took a happy turn during the late-seventeenth and eighteenth centuries.

Children were encouraged early to learn the roles they would later fulfill— kitchen fireplaces with every conceivable accessory (figs. 1.4 and 1.5) honed their culinary skills, and miniature tea and dinner services, produced by

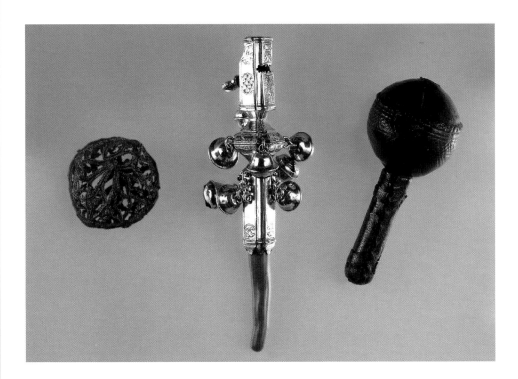

FIGURE 1.1: BABY RATTLES

Considered the baby's first toy, a rattle often reveals the status of parents who eagerly gave their little one a lasting memento of their child's first year. The English rattle on the left, retrieved from the Thames River, dates from the fourteenth century, originally encased small seashells, and was attached to the child's neck by a ribbon. The center rattle, elaborately engraved on silver by William Coles of London, ca. 1735, displays its original coral stem. During the eighteenth century, coral was thought to have mystical properties warding off diseases. On the right, the late-eighteenth-century leather rattle with embossed decorations might reflect a less-expensive approach by an English gentleman to satisfy his young child.

Anne P. and Thomas A. Gray Purchase Fund (hereafter GPF)–4804.9; 4663; 5091

FIGURE 1.2: "HORN BOOKS"

While most toys offer a certain whimsy for children, other toys were educational in design as evidenced by ABC building blocks, or, as here, by "horn books." The seventeenth-century example on the left, retrieved from the Thames River in London, predates the mid-eighteenth-century English "horn book" in the center, which has an actual sheet of horn protecting the handwritten alphabet beneath. Notice the interchanged nature of the letters "i" and "j," as well as "u" and "v." On the right, the brass disk is engraved with its owner's name, James Haws, who lived on the Isle of Wight, England, and turned five years old in 1792.

GPF–5087.9; 4738: 5087.8

every leading English ceramic factory (figs. 1.10 and 1.11), encouraged the tea etiquette of future ladies and gentlemen. Like their parents, young Europeans and Britons also enjoyed the current taste for "all things oriental" with elaborate Chinese export teawares (fig. 1.9a). With such toys, learning could be fun, and only on rare occasions disastrous, evidenced by Hogarth's painting *The Children's Party* (fig. 1.9b)!

"Baby houses" and Dutch collectors cabinets, though predominately in the world of adults, could be prudently played with by children under strict supervision. Expensive silver furnishings and miniature delftwares (figs. 1.7 and 1.8), to be occasionally held and adored by young hands, duplicated a grown-up environment. To date, the earliest recorded dollhouse was created by Albrecht V, Duke of Bavaria, in 1558 for his fortunate daughter. Even though it was destroyed in a tragic fire in 1674, an earlier detailed inventory compiled forty years after its completion gives us a fascinating glimpse into the riches abounding in the house. Four stories tall and decorated by leading artisans of the day, the dollhouse included silver filigree baskets in the wine cellar, a gilt silver parrot cage in the dancing room, and a silver-handled brush and shovel in the day nursery.

Just as sixteenth- and seventeenth-century European children could be lavished sometimes with expensive toys, so too could the family of the first American president. Nelly Custis received from her adopted grandfather, General George Washington, an important paint box (fig. 1.14a), which, remarkably, survives today with its original watercolor paints, and odd props gathered on the Mount Vernon estate. Until acquired by the museum at auction, the paint box had never left the ownership of the Washington family.

But survival, both for children and their toys, was rare in the centuries leading up to the Victorian period, truly the Golden Age of youth and their toys, as we shall see in subsequent chapters.

FIGURE 1.3: EARLY ENGLISH TOYS

The Old Salem Toy Museum possesses the largest collection of archaeologically retrieved English toys outside the Museum of London. The bottom row shows third-century toys of various metals, including small dice, a silver axe, and "shy cocks," or

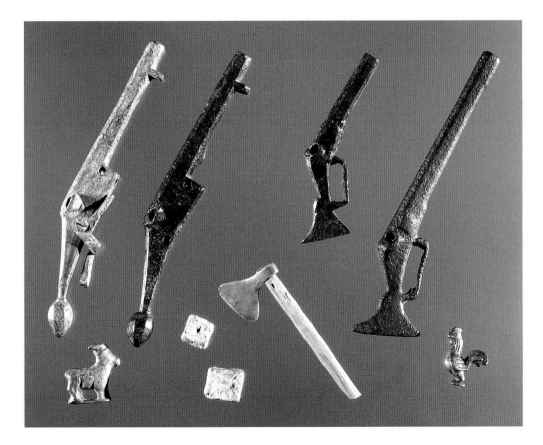

knockover targets for young stone throwers. On the top row are two pistols and two muskets, cast in brass from the Elizabethan period, ca. 1585-1610. Designed with wheel lock or matchlock mechanisms, these toy firearms could actually fire buck shot propelled by tiny charges of gunpowder.

Bottom row: GPF–4815.2; 4813; 4815.3; 4643.1; 4643.2

Top row: GPF–4834.2 and 4834.3 in honor of Jane P. and Earl F. Slick; 5087.4; 4800.7

FIGURE 1.4:
ENGLISH FIREPLACE
WITH CLOCKJACK

Fireplaces, whether included in early English "baby houses" or freestanding like this example, ca. 1715-45, reflect the educational nature of cooking toys for young eighteenth-century children who would one day utilize culinary skills to care for their own children. The fireplace contains a rare spit, or clockjack for roasting meats— a device that apparently disappeared from real kitchens after 1750.

GPF–5049.1-12

FIGURE 1.5:
WROUGHT IRON
FIREGRATE WITH
ACCESSORIES

Doll size in scale and designed for actual cooking, this firegrate with its original wrought iron tools contrasts with the pretend fireplace seen in fig. 1.4. Dating from the mid-eighteenth century in either England or America, the beautifully wrought firegrate is enhanced by an important collection of copper, brass, and iron toy cooking implements, including two late-seventeenth-century earthenware pots and a rare seventeenth-century brass "curfew," preventing sparks from entering the room.

GPF–5087.1-33

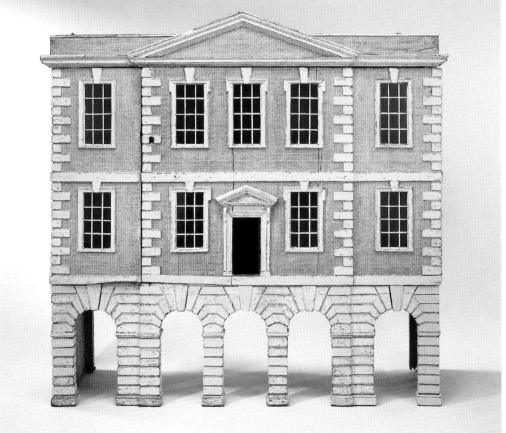

FIGURES 1.6a
AND 1.6b:
GEORGIAN
BABY HOUSE
(interior and exterior)

*This English "baby house,"
ca. 1740-50, may have
been built by an estate
carpenter for a wealthy
family who lived in a similar,
full-scale Palladian-style
country house. The
arcaded base of the house's
exterior simulates the raised
service areas of large
Georgian homes, and the
symmetrically placed
windows and crowning
pediment are typical of
Italian Renaissance architect
Andrea Palladio (1508-80),
whose style saw a revival
in England in the early-
eighteenth century. When
the two hinged doors are
opened, the interior of
this English "baby house"
reveals original paint
treatments, including
graining and marbleizing,
in the splendid paneled
rooms. Two overmantel
oil paintings are signed
"Shuster" and are
attributed to Nuremberg
artist Johann Martin Shuster
(ca. 1667-1738). No other
English "baby house"
of this period contains
overmantel oil paintings.
Evidence of early
illumination in this house
are the ceiling smudge
marks from tiny lighted
candles.*

GPF–4498, in honor of
Frank L. Horton

FIGURE 1.7: ENGLISH SILVER TOYS

Designed as precious furnishings for English "baby houses" of the late-seventeenth and early-eighteenth centuries, silver objects were no doubt valued by aristocratic mothers, who enjoyed the status such objects could offer, and their offspring, who sometimes used the pieces for educational purposes when role-playing for important future household duties. The bowl, tankard, and unique covered colander, ca. 1680-90, were created by the first English silversmith specializing in miniature silver, George Manjoy. A generation later, David Clayton made the plate rack, water kettle on stand, and chocolate pot between 1720-30.

Top row:
GPF–4799; 4802.1;
4876.1-11

Bottom row:
GPF–5046.1; 4796.1; 5046.2

FIGURE 1.8: EUROPEAN AND ORIENTAL MINIATURES

In Holland, well-to-do housewives furnished cabinets with room settings filled with miniature silver, ceramic, brass, and wooden objects—in contrast to English aristocrats and their architectural "baby houses." On the bottom shelf, tin-glazed earthenware objects, referred to as delftwares today, are typical of such cabinet furnishings, including the center punch bowl, dated 1673. The upper shelf includes miniatures (ca. 1690-1720) from China and Japan, whose exports through the Dutch East India Company as early as the fourteenth century to Holland satisfied Imari collectors for "all things oriental."

Top row:
GPF–4801.5; 5085.1; 4824.3

Bottom row:
GPF–5038.1; 4832; 4774

FIGURES 1.9a AND
1.9b: CHINESE EXPORT
TEA SET AND *THE
CHILDREN'S PARTY* BY
WILLIAM HOGARTH

Superbly decorated, this partial tea set from China dates from ca. 1740 period and was originally intended to teach young children tea etiquette. Larger in scale than pieces designed for either Dutch cabinets or English dollhouses, these child-size objects in the "Famille Rose" palette were among the highly prized oriental teawares in demand throughout Europe. The oil painting by William Hogarth (1697-1764), The Children's Party, provides a unique glimpse of aristocratic English children during a disrupted tea party in 1730. Here a family pet turns over a miniature tea table and chairs, which sends the small tea set crashing to the ground. The presence of both miniature furniture and teawares with their young owners in the same painting is proof of the importance of early social training with scaled-down accoutrements.

GPF–5088.1-13 (tea set)
Painting photo courtesy of the National Museum of Wales. © National Museums and Galleries of Wales.

FIGURE 1.10: ENGLISH EIGHTEENTH-CENTURY CHILDREN'S POTTERY

Presented here is a sampling of the Toy Museum's extensive collection of English pottery. Designed between 1740 and 1790, many of these objects were used to educate children in proper tea manners. On the bottom row is a tin-glazed earthenware cup and saucer, attributed to Liverpool, as well as a polychrome saltglaze stoneware teapot, coffeepot, and cup and saucer from the Staffordshire factories, ca. 1760. The top row shows a white saltglaze stoneware coffeepot, a creamware coffeepot and teapot with lead glazes, and an "Astbury-type" teapot, all from the Staffordshire/Derbyshire factories, ca. 1760-85.

Top row: GPF–4852.1; 4782; 5086; 5052.7
Bottom row: GPF–5032.1a-b; 5052.4; 4937.1; 4827.3

FIGURE 1.11: ENGLISH EIGHTEENTH-CENTURY CHILDREN'S PORCELAIN

This representative survey of the museum's important collection of children's soft-paste porcelain, like the children's pottery, was originally intended to teach tea and dinner etiquette. The Caughley factory miniatures on the bottom row are almost small enough to furnish an English "baby house" from the 1780-90 period, especially the rare chamber pot, guglet, and basin on the left. The top row offers four child-size teapots, from 1755 to 1785, made by the Bow, Worcester, Lowestoft, and Pennington factories, all in imitation of earlier Chinese hard-paste teapots designed for future European ladies and gentlemen.

Top row: GPF–5068.1; 5068.2-3; 5078.4; 5078.2; 5078.1

Bottom row: GPF–5068.1-3; 5023.5; 5023.9; 5023.6

FIGURE 1.12: ENGLISH TEA TABLE WITH POTTERY AND SILVER

Only by visualizing children's teawares arranged on a small tea table can visitors truly understand the important role of such pottery in educating young Britons. Here an assembled tea set in the "tortishell" pattern by the Whieldon factories, ca. 1770, are complemented by a hot water kettle by David Clayton, ca. 1720, and a silver gilt tea caddy by Pieter Sommerwill II, ca. 1770. The superbly carved mahogany tea table represents English cabinetmaking during the neoclassical period, ca. 1780-1810.

GPF–5032.4-6 (spoons); 5033 (tongs); 5032.2a-b (silver kettle); 5032.3a-b (tea caddy); 4830.1 (teapot); 4937.2 (pitcher); 5067.1-2 (cups and saucers); 5020.1 (table), gift of Mr. and Mrs. Calder W. Womble, in memory of Ralph P. and DeWitt C. Hanes.

FIGURE 1.13: DR. SAMUEL JOHNSON DINNER SERVICE

This extraordinary miniature dinner service, with its original packing crate and bone cutlery, was a gift to a young girl in London from the famed creator of the first dictionary, Dr. Samuel Johnson (1709-84). Made ca. 1780-84, the pearlware set, stamped "Wedgewood," must have been a prized possession of the family, as attested by its remarkable survival.

GPF–4796.3-35; 4795.2-9; 5018.1-5, in memory of Mallie D. Pepper

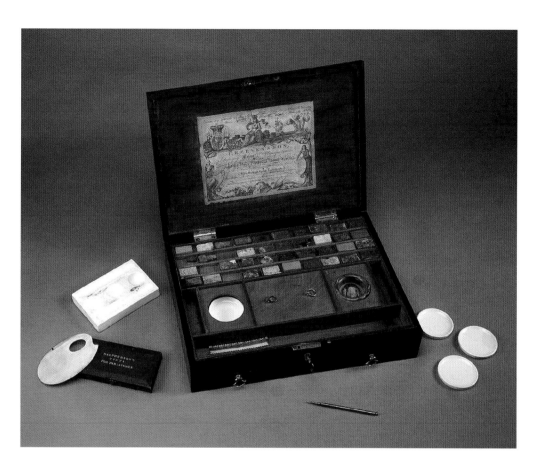

FIGURES 1.14a AND 1.14b: GEORGE WASHINGTON/NELLY CUSTIS PAINT BOX AND PORTRAIT OF WASHINGTON FAMILY BY EDWARD SAVAGE

Historically important, this artist's paint box bears a handwritten inscription by a Custis descendant on the label for T. Reeves & Son, London: "Given by General George Washington to Nelly Custis on her fifteenth birthday, March 31, 1793." The granddaughter of Martha Washington, Eleanor "Nelly" Parke Custis (1779-1852) lived with the first family at Mount Vernon for over twenty years, and affectionately referred to the president as her "Grandpa." Washington recorded in his household accounts the purchase of a box on March 18, 1793: "Pd for a box of paints for Miss Eliza Custis … 3.50 … ." A more likely account entry for this particularly elaborate paint box, on February 17, 1797, might be "30.00" for "a poem and a box of paints for Mrs. W and Miss C …." Edward Savage's ca. 1796 family portrait depicts the seventeen-year-old Nelly, her brother, George Washington Parke Custis, the president, and Mrs. Washington. Martha Washington points with her fan to a map of the "Capital City" then being developed on the banks of the Potomac River, sixteen miles from Mount Vernon. Already an accomplished musician and artist when this image was painted, Nelly continued these pursuits when she built "Woodlawn," a plantation adjacent to Mount Vernon.

GPF–5084.1-21 (paint box), in memory of Anne P. Gray (1921-2003)

The Washington Family by Edward Savage reproduced courtesy of the Andrew W. Mellon Collection, National Gallery of Art, Washington, DC. Image ©2004 Board of Trustees, National Gallery of Art, Washington, DC.

CHAPTER 2
DOLLHOUSES AND ROOMBOXES

FOR children, the nineteenth century was the "Golden Age" of toys and dollhouses. No longer were young ones relegated to distant nurseries, overprotected from the ever-present diseases prevalent during earlier times, or rarely allowed to play in their mothers' world of elaborate "baby houses" or collectors' cabinets filled with sparkling miniature silver, imported and precious tiny oriental vases, as well as Dutch delftwares.

With Queen Victoria's ascension to the throne in 1837, major changes in social mores slowly took shape, and children became integral members of the family hierarchy. Queen Victoria (1819-1901), in fact, regularly presented children in her court with gifts of dollhouses, furnished in the latest Biedermeier taste. Even with the Victorian period's concept of rigid morality and manners, children from mercantile and wealthy families were constantly encouraged to play with dollhouses and "Nuremberg kitchens," playthings to properly prepare children for household duties ahead.

This era of mass production allowed for toys, including dollhouses, to be designed and built for children of all economic levels. In a real sense, London's Great Exhibition of 1851 was a celebration of mass production. Victorians also relished new printing techniques, especially chromolithography, which made complex printed wallpapers, inlaid floors, and fashionable veneers cheaply available to all toymakers.

Hand-made "baby houses" of the eighteenth century became scarce during the nineteenth century as toymakers realized the profit potential of mass-produced dollhouses with chromolithographed paper veneers. Ludwig Moritz Gottschalk (1840-1905) of Marienberg, Germany, founded his company in 1865 and became a leader in mass-produced, but hand-finished, "blue roof" and later "red roof" dollhouses (fig. 2.3). After his death, his family continued the proud Gottschalk tradition until 1942.

Christian Hacker, whose Thuringia firm was founded in Germany in 1850, was another clever designer. The houses of Gottschalk and Hacker were often designed appropriately for French, English, or American tastes (figs. 2.2a and 2.2b), and were exported throughout the world. English makers, such

FIGURES 2.1a AND 2.1b: ENGLISH REGENCY-STYLE DOLLHOUSE
(interior and exterior)

This splendid house, reminiscent of a London row house, ca. 1860, is enhanced by original hand-painted wallpapers, velvet rugs, grained doors and staircase, and silk draperies with lace curtains. Key furnishings to note are the lithographed parlor set, the Märklin photographic carousel in the gentlemen's study, and the built-in Evans & Cartwright kitchen stove. In the early-nineteenth century, Evans & Cartwright of Wolverhampton became the center in Britain for the manufacture of tinplate toys, providing fireplaces, insert stoves, and miniature furniture with distinctive orange-brown graining. While the furniture here, and in the other Victorian dollhouses, is not original to each particular house, the furnishings are exceptional and appropriate for the nineteenth-century period.

GPF–4945

as Silber and Fleming, and American firms like R. Bliss Manufacturing Company of Rhode Island, while prolific in their marketing, competed as best they could with the German leaders of the industry.

New technologies also enabled dollhouse furniture makers in Germany to move from handmade toys in the eighteenth century to "production-made" toys in the nineteenth. stablished in the late-eighteenth century, the firm of Babette Schweitzer in Diessen continues today with its quality cast pewter, filigree dollhouse furniture. The finishes of its furniture are generally gold, silver, or asphalten, a dark-brown glaze resembling walnut. As early as 1804, the firm of Rock and Graner of Biberacher Blechspielzeug, Germany, produced cannons, coaches, ships, trains, and its trademark lacquered and then painted tinplate dollhouse furniture. The hand-soldered miniature furniture is distinguished by dark-brown grained colors simulating mahogany or rosewood, as well as support brackets cast in the shape of serpents. Rock and Graner became a leader in the field during the 1850s, but the firm was dissolved by 1904.

Another extremely prolific manufacturing firm producing wooden dollhouse furniture, was Gebrüder Schneegaas and Son of Waltershausen, Germany. Founded in the 1830s, Schneegaas adeptly designed in the popular Biedermeier, gothic revival, rococo, and empire styles, and is widely collected today. Their furniture is often upholstered in purple or blue silk and is trimmed with narrow gilt paper impressed with a beaded pattern.

If Schneegaas led the world during the nineteenth century with wooden pieces, then Gebrüder Märklin of Göppingen, Germany, was the premier manufacturer of tinplate toys in Europe since its founding in 1840. Maintaining preeminence in the field of toy trains, Märklin first manufac-

FIGURE 2.2a:
CHRISTIAN HACKER
HOUSE (exterior)

Created in Nuremberg, Germany, ca. 1895-1910, by Christian Hacker, this late Victorian dollhouse displays its original, hand-painted wallpapers and lace curtains, and is labeled by the Hacker firm "no. 422\2."

GPF–4944

tured toys for dollhouse kitchens in 1859, later moving into "floor-running" locomotives and railway stations, as well as superbly modeled metal dollhouse furniture, usually finished with gold gilt.

Germany remained the leader of dollhouse furniture and accessory manufacturing until the beginning of World War I. Post-World War I, embargos and nationalistic fervor restricted the exportation of dollhouse miniatures so prevalent a decade earlier. While only a sample of the museum's dollhouses and roomboxes are pictured here, superb examples of Schneegaas, Gottschalk, Rock and Graner, Schweitzer, and Märklin can be found throughout the collection.

Like dollhouses, roomboxes are virtual microcosms of adult life in Victorian nineteenth century (figs. 2.4 through 2.9). Children today can discover the technologies of an earlier era, finding an intriguing evolution of plumbing, lighting, and transportation from a time when advances in technology were rapid and dramatic. Historians, who long have regarded oil paintings as "windows" into the Victorian Age, now relish dollhouses and roomboxes with period furnishings as a more three-dimensional, detailed depiction of true nineteenth-century lifestyles.

FIGURE 2.2b: CHRISTIAN HACKER HOUSE (interior)

Inside, a varied and important collection of grained, tinplate furniture by Rock and Graner, Biberacher Blechspielzeug, Germany, is complemented by Simon & Halbig dolls—including rare gentleman and lady golfers dressed in their original clothing and accessories.

GPF–4944

FIGURE 2.3: GOTTSCHALK HOUSE; BLISS HOUSE AND STABLE

Typical of the half-timbered and brick lithographed dollhouses by Ludwig Moritz Gottschalk,

this house has all the vocabulary of an 1870 Queen Anne structure. Referred to by modern collectors as a "blue roof" house because of its unusual roof color outlined by black striping, the house appears in Gottschalk's 1885 toy catalog as "no. 3587." To the right of the inviting house are a stable and house by R. Bliss of Rhode Island, completing this picturesque streetscape.

GPF–4865.5; 4689.1; 4570.5

FIGURE 2.4: GROCERY STORE

This grocery store, with its typical cream-colored woodwork by Ludwig Moritz Gottschalk of Marienberg, Germany, was created between 1880 and 1890. Particularly noteworthy are the original contents, including sugar cones, wooden vases and bottles, and pewter labels for the English-speaking market. Two dolls by Simon & Halbig, ca. 1880, are engrossed in business, or possibly flirtation!

GPF–4551.8-9; 4570.21-22

FIGURE 2.5: EDWARDIAN MILLINERY SHOP

Also by Gottschalk, this elegant hat shop would have been the envy of every young girl in 1880.   How easy it would be for her to imagine shopping for each of the original hats and fancy boxes in this Marienberg, Germany, boutique. The lady doll, dressed in her original lace finery by Simon & Halbig of Thuringia, Germany, sports her own elaborate hat, perhaps purchased in the shop on an earlier visit.

GPF–5034.1, in memory of DeWitt C. and Ralph P. Hanes

FIGURE 2.6: TOBACCO SHOP

Attributed to the Rock and Graner firm of Biberacher Blechspielzeug, Germany, ca. 1840-50, this architectural tour de force is unique with its marbleized columns, grained cabinets, and Dresden paper decals. Complete with its original tobacco products, cigars bound with paper labels, and humidors, the shop only lacks the original plaster proprietor mounted on a disc which could be moved by the wooden knob mounted in the front base. Two gentlemen dolls by Simon & Halbig, ca. 1880 from Germany, appear pleased with the purchases underway.

GPF–5034.2, in memory of James A. Gray Jr.

FIGURE 2.7: BUTCHER SHOP

Like a number of roomboxes in the collection, this butcher shop was made by Gottschalk,

ca. 1870, and numbered 647. With its distinctive patterned floor and marbleized woodwork, the butcher shop comes with its original beef and pork cuts hanging throughout the shop. To shelter young shoppers from the gruesome sight of freshly slaughtered meat, piles of appealing vegetables are strategically placed on counters to make the experience more pleasurable. Children would be expected to recognize specific cuts of meat after playing with this educational toy.

GPF–5061.1-42

FIGURE 2.8: KITCHEN AND LAUNDRY

This kitchen and laundry contrasts with the Nuremberg kitchen shown in fig. 2.9 and displays a fifty-year progression in implements, a cooking stove by Märklin, and a more modern approach to laundering. From the 1890 to 1910 period, this double roombox attributed to Gottschalk is distinguished by a vast array of original contents, and particularly noteworthy is the freshly pressed laundry bound with paper ribbons denoting its designated bedroom.

GPF–4502.44-55

FIGURE 2.9: NUREMBERG KITCHEN

One of two in the Old Salem Toy Museum collection, this "Nuremberg kitchen" remarkably contains its original copper, brass, and steel furnishings, all ca. 1850. The toy is given this name because Nuremberg was the center of the European trade of that time, and because these toy kitchens resembled the real kitchens of southern Germany. Usually these roomboxes have a central cooking hearth with wood storage below and a hood above, a checkered floor, shelves for plates, many hooks for hanging utensils, and a poultry pen. Such Nuremberg kitchens became popular as learning toys in the seventeenth century and continued to be made into the twentieth century.

GPF–4739.3

CHAPTER 3
ZOOS, MENAGERIES, AND CIRCUSES

INTEREST in the "exotic," whether they were plants, animals, or people, abounded in the nineteenth century. Of special interest to children were the new public zoos, where anyone could see wonderful animals from all parts of the globe. It is no wonder that these animals and their surroundings were the inspiration for children's toys in the forms of miniature zoos and menageries that could be enjoyed at home.

Adding to the excitement were the popular circuses, where exotic creatures performed with equally exotic people and clowns under the "Big Top" tents to provide memorable entertainment. Even in Salem, North Carolina, the children saw a "most remarkable event" in 1807—an elephant. By the 1830s, traveling circuses frequently visited the area.

In response to these new curiosities, toymakers in Germany, as well as German-born toymakers who had immigrated to America, began making circuses, zoos, and menageries with interchangeable animals, so children could maintain that enchanting memory of a circus visit. In the Toy Museum there are toys that youngsters cherished as reminders of their first sight of a lumbering elephant parading down Main Street or an amusement ride high above the sights, sounds, and smells of a circus tent far below.

Pop-up books heightened the excitement of reading for young Victorians during the last decades of the nineteenth century. Lothar Meggendorfer (1847-1925), considered a master of mechanical books, is lauded for his humor and artistic talents in the era, which cherished the sixty or more books he created in Esslingen, Germany. His "International Circus" (fig. 3.1) stands as his most ambitious work.

American and German manufacturers created a wide variety of circus toys (fig. 3.2), which were enjoyed as souvenirs of visits to circuses the world over. After the turn of the twentieth century, Albert Schoenhut (1849-1912), born in Württemberg, Germany, was a third-generation dollmaker who immigrated to Philadelphia at age seventeen, and soon added wooden circus toys, in 1903, to his manufacture of musical instruments, blocks, dolls, and dollhouses. His "Humpty-Dumpty Circus" (fig. 3.4a) became his most famous creation, and before the company closed its doors in 1935, Schoenhut was recognized as a major exporter from the United States. His circuses with hand-painted performers were loved and appreciated throughout the world.

The popularity of Schoenhut's circuses occurred during a period that saw circuses come to the forefront of American entertainment. The performers and exotic animals also mirrored the dazzling success of Barnum and Bailey, and the separate Ringling Brothers, circuses. By 1918, when the two circuses merged, the A. Schoenhut Company stood at the pinnacle of circus toymaking.

Menageries and zoological gardens, on the other hand, have a distinguished career extending from the days of the Romans and Greeks. More recently, the first public zoo occurred during the heyday of the French Revolution, opening in 1793 as the "Jardin des Plantes," successor to the Royal Zoo at Versailles. Menageries or public zoos followed: the Zoological Garden of London (1828), the gardens in Amsterdam (1843), and New York's Central Park (1862). Unfortunately, throughout these parks little attention was given to the health and welfare of the animals, but rather the ensembles were created for human amusement and symbols of status and power. In no way did these municipal attractions mirror the enlightened zoos of today.

Though successful as a toy, "Barnums Great Menagerie" (fig. 3.3) is more a reflection of the showmanship of Phineas T. Barnum and the cruelly caged animals gawked at by city dwellers. When Barnum housed his circus animals in the Central Park menagerie during the 1890s, the commercial entertainment was criticized by Central Park commissioners, who begged for the animals to be moved from their ill-arranged and ill-equipped houses to the new Bronx Zoo.

Regardless of the realities posed by the zoos, menageries, and circuses of the nineteenth century, these enterprises brought hours of delight to Victorians who were awed by the unusual and the exotic. Today, we admire the toymakers who miniaturized their perfect sense of wonderment.

FIGURE 3.1: *GRAND CIRQUE INTERNATIONAL*

One of the largest and most complex mechanical books created by Lothar Meggendorfer is the "International Circus." Published by J.F. Schreiber of Esslingen, Germany, in 1887, the pop-up book is over 52 inches in length, with 450 individually drawn people in the audience. Created in several languages, our rare example was published for the French market.

GPF–4748

FIGURE 3.2:
CIRCUS TOYS

Toymakers were quick to replicate the circus rides and wagons that Victorian children encountered each year as various troupes traveled to their towns and villages. This important group of tinplate toys includes an impressive merry-go-round by Märklin, ca. 1905; "Barnum's Menagerie" lion wagon by Merriam Manufacturing Company, Durham, Connecticut, ca. 1880; a platform camel and rider by Althof, Bergmann and Company, New York, ca. 1870; and a circus wagon by Francis, Field, and Francis, Philadelphia, ca. 1850.

GPF–4570.4; 4733.2; 4723; 4507.4

FIGURE 3.3: "BARNUM'S GREAT MENAGERIE"

Like so many German toys created by unidentified toymakers, "Barnum's Great Menagerie" was destined for the English-speaking world, as evidenced by the hand-painted sign and American flags atop the menagerie. Cleverly designed with a sliding platform below the principal structure, the toy includes a number of original elastolin animals, which were molded from flour, glue, and fillers, and then hand painted ca. 1895-1910.

GPF–4502.65

FIGURES 3.4a and 3.4b: "HUMPTY-DUMPTY CIRCUS" WITH ORIGINAL BOX TOP

Created by a first-generation German immigrant to America, Albert Schoenhut introduced the first three pieces of his most famous creation, the "Humpty-Dumpty Circus," in 1903 from his Philadelphia factory. Only a few of the sixty-three pieces of the circus are illustrated here. The Schoenhut circus displayed in the Toy Museum is the most complete collection on public view. It includes many glass-eyed animals from the early period, as well as the elaborate and rare parade wagons introduced in 1910. Hidden elastic bands allowed the toy animals and performers to be bent or contorted in every conceivable position. The colorful original box top aptly alludes to the excitement and adventure to be found inside.

GPF–4502.56-59

FIGURE 3.5: PUNCH AND JUDY THEATER

A favorite of visitors, our Punch and Judy theater with its original puppets dates from the 1830-40 period from the Erzebirge region of Germany. Just as circuses provided staged entertainment for children of all ages, so Punch and Judy theaters were set up at fairs and public gatherings to tell the fascinating story of Punch, who, as a hand puppet, could step beyond reality, flaunt petty authority, and become a great spokesman for liberty and equality. From the original text dating from 1828, Punch's aversions are the Landlord, the Judge, the Hangman, Death, the Policeman, and, occasionally, even his wife.

GPF–4502.37

CHAPTER 4
DOLLS AND PARLOR TOYS

IF the eighteenth century was a time of political independence through armed revolution, then the nineteenth century could be considered the dawn of material independence through the industrial revolution. In America, the civilization along the Atlantic coastline became a continental empire. Millions of acres of virgin land and abundant resources at every man's fingertips brought manufacturing, commerce, and transportation, meaning prosperity for families, more complex toys and amusements for their children, and a consumptive society never seen before.

Dolls might be seen as a microcosm of these changes in American and European lifestyles. The doll seen in fig. 4.1 might represent the insular world of late-seventeenth-century London, where individual toymakers turned their wooden dolls' heads on lathes and painted the prim faces with little individuality. By the 1870s, German dollmakers like Simon & Halbig exported African American bisque heads to the United States. Students at the Hampton Normal and Agricultural Institute, in Hampton, Virginia, the first school for African Americans in this nation, founded in 1868, dressed the two Simon & Halbig dolls now in the Toy Museum's collection with pride and endearment (fig. 4.2).

The first doll in North Carolina—and for that matter the first toy in the New World—was recorded far earlier. Commenting in 1585 on the Roanoke Island expedition, John White illustrated an Indian squaw and child holding her Elizabethan doll, dressed in the latest fashion with ruff and lace. Through gestures of friendship and barter, the Indians were offered:

> glasses, knives, babies [meaning dolls] and other trifles, which we though [sic] they delighted in. Soe [sic] they stood still, and perveringe our Good will and courtesie came fawning upon us, and bade us welcome.

Wealthy aristocrats on both sides of the Atlantic bought the first French fashion dolls for their children. Representing the pinnacle of nineteenth-century sophistication, such fashion dolls were accompanied by custom wardrobes and every imaginable accessory, as witnessed by "Lillie" in fig. 4.5.

Automatons represented the cutting-edge technologies evident in France and Germany during the mid-nineteenth century, and trace their origins to the mechanical advances found in cathedral and town clocks across Europe from Medieval times. Amusements for children of all ages, the four automatons in the Toy Museum are elegant cousins of French fashion dolls, but differ from the dolls by moving in a most lifelike manner when wound (fig. 4.7). The automatons might stand at the zenith of Victorian dollmaking expertise, especially when compared to the one-of-a-kind side hill plow with oxen (fig. 4.6) or the two-dimensional paper doll "Little Henry" (fig. 4.9).

The Old Salem Toy Museum also exhibits an important collection of miniature furniture, scaled to the dolls enjoyed in both America and England. Fig. 4.3, though primarily made up of London-made examples in the leading styles of the eighteenth century, represents the exceptional skills of cabinetmakers called on by aristocrats and their children, eager for harmonious furniture to accompany their wood-headed and papier-mâché dolls. While one will never know for sure if these veneered pieces were originally intended as purely salesmen's samples or actual accessories for dolls—we favor the latter consideration. The large number of miniature pieces extant, as well as the wealth available, primarily in Europe, to commission both adult- and doll-size furniture for a family and their children, must weigh heavily in any debate on this issue.

With the dawn of the "Gilded Age" in America, about 1870, and the increased leisure time for the middle classes, parlor games promoted "togetherness" for the

FIGURE 4.1a AND 4.1b: JAMES II SHEPHERDESS DOLL AND DUTCH PRINT OF DOLL PURCHASE

The earliest doll in our collection and a rare survival from the James II period, the shepherdess doll, ca. 1685, comes complete with her original bonnet and crook. Like

many late-seventeenth-century dolls, she in encased is her original shadowbox, which certainly helped preserve the delicate fabrics and wood head, arms, and feet, all displaying a high level of craftsmanship. English examples from this period were lathe turned and hand finished, and were distinguished by high foreheads, as well as wide almond-shaped eyes and a prim expression. The page from a Dutch book, ca. 1650, depicts in the engraving a mother and eager daughter purchasing an early, wood-headed doll, not unlike the shepherdess doll shown in fig. 4.1a.

GPF–4894.1 (doll), in memory of Gordon Hanes, and in honor of Helen C. Hanes; and 5150.3 (print)

FIGURE 4.2: HAMPTON INSTITUTE DOLLS

African American dolls from the second half of the nineteenth century are rare, especially this pair with heads by Simon & Halbig of Thuringia, Germany, and clothes, ca. 1880, by students at the

Hampton Normal and Agricultural Institute in Hampton, Virginia. The Institute was founded in 1868 to prepare young African American men and women as leaders and teachers of their newly freed people. The laundry rack, tinplate tub by George Brown of Forrestville, Connecticut, and the goose by S. Gunthermann of Nuremberg, Germany, all date ca. 1870-90.

GPF–4502.22

family, adults, and children. Sisters Catherine Beecher and Harriet Beecher Stowe cleanly advocated "family diversions" in their 1869 book *The American Woman's Home*:

Another example for family diversion is to be found in the various games played by children, and in which the joining of older members of the family is always a great advantage to both parties.

While some card games, board games, and puzzles depended on mere chance, others honed mental and manual skills. These parlor games, as seen in figs. 4.10 and 4.11a, often were not mere pastimes, they were shared educational activities for parents and their children and promoted moral and religious messages, as well as teaching other topics such as geography, literature, and financial acumen.

Optical toys, as represented in fig. 4.10, peep shows, panoramas, and sound toys amazed children when these devices first became popular at the end of the eighteenth century. Because many of the toys involved objects that could be transformed into something else, as if by magic, they became know as "metamorphoses." Also, "speaking books," a German creation, mechanically reproduced sounds of farm animals for additional delight.

In the eighteenth and nineteenth centuries, children's play on Sunday was limited, but certain toys that promoted religious or moralistic themes sometimes were allowed. Children in Salem, North Carolina, for instance, were admonished for playing marbles, ball games, flying a kite, hunting and shooting, or swimming on Sunday. In 1794, the church records note: "We wished our young people would spend the rest of their time [on Sunday] with something useful. To read a book is a good way of spending one's time." Noah's arks and Sunday school block toys by the Bliss Manufacturing Company of

FIGURE 4.3: ENGLISH DOLL-SCALE FURNITURE

The Old Salem Toy Museum owns an important collection of doll-scale, miniature furniture, created primarily in England, ca. 1720-1860. Shown here is a group displaying exquisite craftsmanship, with harmonious proportions, detailed dovetailing, original brass pulls, and extraordinary inlays and walnut veneers. Clockwise from the upper left are a serpentine commode (ca. 1775), a walnut veneered kneehole desk (ca. 1740), an inlaid gentleman's clothes press (ca. 1735), a walnut armchair (ca. 1720), and a unique polychrome architect's table (ca. 1760). It does not take much imagination to envision English aristocratic or royal children placing their dolls among such specialized furniture!

GPF–5099.1-28

Pawtucket, Rhode Island, escaped this parental criticism.

A theatrical parlor toy is *Pollock's Juvenile Drama*, (fig. 4.12), dating circa 1880. Complete with all scenery and guides for the young aspiring actors who originally owned the theater, the toy was created by Benjamin Pollock of London, who in 1877 married the daughter of John Redington (1819-76), owner of a well-established printing and stationery business. The toy theaters in Redington's line were continued by Pollock, with his improvements, for over sixty years, and are today considered small, hand-colored masterpieces by toy collectors the world over.

Marbles are culturally important — they brought children together in social settings from early centuries to the 1950s (fig. 4.13). Marbles have been around for over 5,000 years. They are made of many different materials, such as stone, semi-precious minerals, wood, metals, glass, and clays. Marbles were made by potters in Salem, North Carolina, and were also a tremendous source of income for glass manufacturers in Lauscha, Germany, from the mid 1800s to the mid 1900s.

FIGURE 4.4: DOLL-SIZE "GREAT CHAIRS"

Recent additions to the Toy Museum are two American "great chairs," ca. 1750, from Bergen County, New Jersey or the southern New York State area. Each chair is slightly over eight inches tall. The design of the turned armchair harkens back to spindle-back examples made by Dutch artisans in New Amsterdam (now New York City) as early as 1640. While our two chairs embody decorative traits from surviving adult-sized seating furniture of the early eighteenth century, these chairs qualify as doll's chairs because of their scale.

GPF–5146 (side chair); and 5139 (armchair), in honor of Robert F. Trent

FIGURE 4.5: "LILLIE" FRENCH FASHION DOLL WITH TROUSSEAU

Our French fashion doll "Lillie" is so named because of her engraved calling card. With her porcelain head, kid leather body, and complete original trousseau, ca. 1870, the doll reflects the epitome of French fashion and culture during the twenty-two year reign of Napoleon III and his beloved wife, Empress Eugenie. By 1867, there were more than two hundred shops in Paris specializing in the component body parts of fashion dolls, to say nothing of the boutiques offering every conceivable accessory to dress and glamorize the dolls with personalized trunks, fans, writing utensils, and gloves. Like most fashion dolls, our example is not labeled nor signed due to the many seamstresses and artisans involved with her creation. In addition to the items shown here, the Toy Museum is privileged to possess six other complete outfits for "Lillie," including a full-length woolen bathing suit.

GPF–4650; 4630.2-5; in honor of Ann Crews Ring

FIGURE 4.6: SIDE HILL PLOW, WITH FARMER DOLL

Probably a unique creation, this side hill plow, with wheels and oxen of varying size, reflects a traditional "folk art" approach to toymaking. A local craftsman made the toy, as opposed to a professional toymaker who often mass produced more detailed toys. From Schoharie

County, New York, the plow and oxen date ca. 1870. The farmer doll, part of the Dressel 1896 portrait series, was originally owned in Salem, North Carolina, by members of the Vogler and Fries families. Attributed to Roullet & Decamps of Paris, the pig automaton with clockwork mechanism dates ca. 1870-90.

GPF–4730; 4785; 4502.27

FIGURE 4.7: AUTOMATONS

These four automatons are descendents of the elaborate mechanical toys that were the eighteenth-century playthings of European royalty. Primarily made in Germany and France, they served as amusements, but they were also examples of a country's mechanical technology. From the left are a lady spinning by J.D. Kestner (Waltershausen, Germany, ca. 1840), "Little Girl with Broken Punch" (Leopold Lambert, Paris, ca. 1890), lady with a harp (Sonneberg area, Germany, ca. 1865), and "Wild Bill Hickcock" (J. Théroude, Paris, ca. 1860).

GPF–4570.18; 4541.1 ("Little Girl with Broken Punch") gift of Mr. and Mrs. F. Borden Hanes Jr.; 4551.6; 4551.2

FIGURE 4.8:
TEDDY BEARS

Children of all ages can identify with the teddy bear. An avid sportsman, President Theodore Roosevelt enjoyed hunting black bears in Mississippi but drew the line on one unsuccessful hunt in 1902 when he refused to shoot a tethered bear his guides had captured and offered as an easy kill for the president. News spread quickly and a commemorative toy was born. Sitting beside the American velocipede is a mohair teddy bear by an early maker, Margarete Steiff, ca. 1908, from Giengen an der Brenz, Germany. Seated on the riding toy is a second mohair

bear by Steiff, ca. 1904-05, and a small bear by Schreyer and Co. (Schuco Trademark), Nuremberg, Germany, ca. 1910-15. The small bear has a "yes/no" lever in its back to move the bear's head to indicate approval with a nod or disapproval with a turn of his head.

GPF–4672.8; 4691; 4688; 3720.1

FIGURE 4.9: "LITTLE HENRY" PAPER DOLL

"Little Henry" was the first commercial paper doll published for children. With hand-colored engravings, the book and paper doll date to 1810 and have their original slipcase. A moral tale, the story of "Little Henry" traces the kidnapping of Henry and his colorful life. Henry was followed by other two-dimensional dolls from S. & J. Fuller and their "Temple of Fancy" in London, England.

GPF–4571.1

FIGURE 4.10: OPTICAL TOYS

In the Toy Museum there are a number of optical toys, often considered the forerunners of animation. On the left, "The Magic Mirror, or Wonderful Transformations" by McLoughlin Brothers, New York, ca. 1880, was one of the most popular optical toys of the nineteenth century. Reflected in the conical mirror is a clear picture recreated from the distorted image on the cardboard beneath it. On the right, the zoetrope by Milton Bradley of Springfield, Massachusetts, ca. 1867, produced a "moving picture" seen through slits in the drum, which, when spun on its wooden base, offered an optical illusion similar to early animated cartoons.

GPF–4502.4; 4502.38

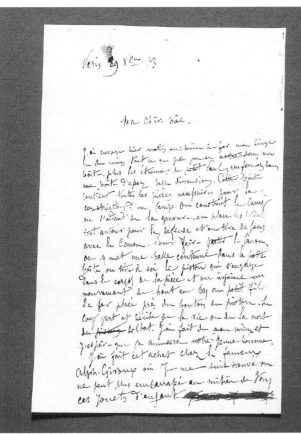

FIGURES 4.11a AND 4.11b:
EPISODE DE LA GUERRE D'AFRIQUE AND LETTER DESCRIBING THE TOY'S PURCHASE

The dream of every toy collector is to find a parlor toy with an accompanying document originally presenting the toy. Here, a young French girl's letter describes buying the Episode de la Guerre d'Afrique at a leading Parisian toy store in 1874 as a gift for her younger brother. With a hand-colored lid, building-block castle, and soldiers, the game includes the original cannons, all ready for a parlor game of war.

GPF–4567.1

FIGURE 4.12: *POLLOCK'S JUVENILE DRAMA*

As early as 1811, toymakers in England printed and hand colored children's theaters, complete with scenery, actors, props, scripts, and directions for manipulating the figures and creating sound effects like thunder and cannon blasts. Our theater by Benjamin Pollock (1856-1937), dating from 1880, is remarkably complete, including its original packing crate and numerous sets and scripts, like Sleeping Beauty in the Woods *depicted here. For over sixty years Pollock printed his juvenile drama sets for English children eager to recreate popular theatrical plays.*

GPF–4502.35

FIGURE 4.13: MARBLES

With a history tracing their origins to 6000 BCE, marbles can be considered one of the first games ever played by children. The collection of marbles at the Toy Museum is a survey of the most desirable forms. These examples were primarily produced in Lauscha, Germany, between 1890 and 1910. Of particular note are the sulphide marbles: clear glass spheres that encase white or silvery figures of pipe clay. The display at the museum is backlit by fiber optics, producing a dramatic effect reminiscent of a heavenly solar system.

GPF–4692.1-18

CHAPTER 5
SALEM, NORTH CAROLINA, TOYS

THE cornerstone of the Old Salem Toy Museum is a remarkable collection of toys owned by children in Salem, North Carolina. Most were made in Germany during the nineteenth century, and the Moravians honored their heritage by purchasing toys from their homeland.

German toys—made of wood, metal, papier-mâché, or glass—were known the world over for their excellent craftsmanship, appealing design, colorful appearance, and inexpensive price. So many toys were made in or sold through Nuremberg, an international trading center since the fifteenth century, that German toys in general became known as "Nuremberg" toys, regardless of their town of origin. These toys were exported all over Europe, and by the early nineteenth century reached America, principally through the ports of New York, Philadelphia, Baltimore, or Charleston. Some "Nuremberg" toys were even ordered directly from Germany for the children at Salem (fig. 5.1).

There have been children in Salem since the first families moved into the new town in 1771. Although a good deal is known about family life and the education of boys and girls in the Salem schools, little is known about their leisure-time playthings until the early-nineteenth century. The first written record of toys in Salem, from 1785, only says "one green tin box with playthings," and gives no further explanation.

In 1804, however, the descriptions become more specific, and ties to the German toy industry are evident when the Small Wares Shop on Salem Square received "one box of Nührnberg [sic] toys." As time went on, other types of toys were recorded, such as play wagons, toy books, dolls, paint boxes, marbles, and children's chairs. By the 1870s, the toys available in Salem rivaled those found in other towns its size, and newspaper advertisements and painted broadsides announced enchanted lists of playthings that would have delighted any child.

Some toys were made locally, and luckily have been donated to Old Salem by descendants of the original owners. The Salem Pottery in the early-nineteenth century produced and sold a variety of colorfully glazed earthenware toys including "dolls" and "toy birds, dogs, and sheep." Salem potters, including Henry Shaffner (1798-1877) and John Holland (1781-1843) are represented in the Toy Museum, as well as cabinetmakers like Friedrich Belo (1780-1827) who created miniature furniture (fig. 5.3). A number of charming children's portraits exist from the Salem painter Daniel Welfare

FIGURES 5.1a AND 5.1b: SALEM-OWNED TOYS

Old Salem is certainly lucky to exhibit a number of German-made toys once owned by Salem children throughout the nineteenth century. From the Erzgebirge region of Germany, the Noah's ark was a first birthday present for Francis Levin Fries (1812-63), and the ink description on the bottom reads: "Frank Fries. Presented to his father when he was one year old. Oct. 17th. 1813." Also from the Erzgebirge region are men working a wood plane, and the cow, horse, and sheep pull toys, ca. 1860. From the Sonneberg region of Germany come the rooster and cat squeak toys—toys that sit on a small bellows and make a squeaking sound when compressed, much to the delight of children. The dollhouse furniture pieces by Gebrüder Schneegaas of Waltershausen, Germany, ca. 1890-1900, are remarkable survivors of the Biedermeier style and were originally owned by Margaret Blair McCuiston (1894-1994).

354.37 (Noah's ark)
Top Row: 567; 4952, C-136;
S-165, C-137, 430.43
Bottom Row: GPF– 4917.1-11

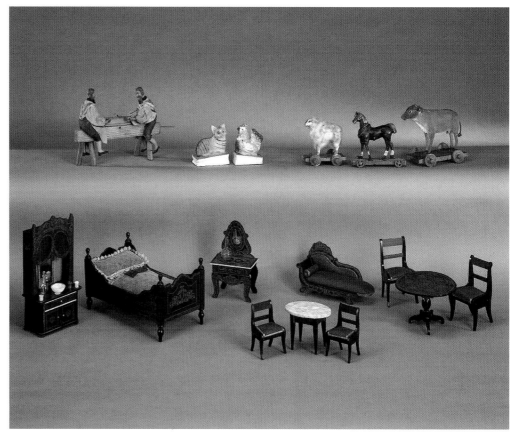

(1796-1841), and these hang throughout the museum and in Old Salem exhibition buildings (fig. 5.3).

By the end of the nineteenth century and the beginning of the twentieth century, dollmakers in Salem produced some of the most endearing toys that we display today. The Pfohl sisters, Margaret Gertrude and Caroline Elizabeth, and their mentor Emma Chitty, first made cardboard patterns for their dolls and paper patterns for the dolls' clothes (figs. 5.2 and 5.3). Daguerreotypes of Salem children—proudly holding their "Maggie Bessie" and "Miss Chitty" dolls, as well as German toys purchased locally—survive. Many of these images were captured by Henry A. Lineback, a professional photographer in Salem for over fifty years, and a sampling can be seen in the Toy Museum.

FIGURE 5.2: "MAGGIE BESSIE" DOLLS

Distinctive cloth dolls made in Salem by sisters Margaret Gertrude (1877-1965) and Caroline Elizabeth Pfohl (1870-1959) for over fifty years became known as "Maggie Bessie" dolls. According to their 1897-1916 account book, the two sisters, by 1916, had made 435 dolls. The three "Maggie Bessie" dolls pictured here include a rare boy doll and a miniature doll, part of the only known complete "Maggie Bessie" family for a dollhouse.

2935, given by Dr. Roy Truslow in memory of Caroline W. Gray Truslow; 3204.2 (miniature doll); 4877 (boy doll), on loan from Hamilton C. Horton

FIGURE 5.3:
"MISS CHITTY" DOLL

While "Maggie Bessie" dolls are cherished by collectors today, "Miss Chitty" dolls are considered even more rare. The Pfohl sisters most likely learned their craft from Salem friend and dollmaker Emma Chitty (1848-1919). The cherry and poplar blanket chest, ca. 1820, is attributed to the Salem cabinetmaker Friedrich Belo, while the slip-decorated earthenware teapot, cup, and saucer were most likely made by potter Henry Shaffner in Salem, ca. 1825. The charming portrait of the Samuel Schultz children, ca. 1831, is by Salem painter Daniel Welfare.

2069.1; T-182; 234; D-191

FIGURE 5.4:
"CHRISTMAS TOYS!"
BROADSIDE

The informative broadside at the Winston Republican newspaper offices in Winston, North Carolina, ca. 1880, advertises many types of toys available to the townspeople of "Salem-Winston." C.A. Winkler (1858-93) was the proprietor of a bakery and confectionery shop on Main Street near Old Shallowford Road in Salem.

Reproduced courtesy of Moravian Archives, Winston-Salem, North Carolina.

CHAPTER 6
GERMAN WOODEN TOYS

THE most extensive single collection in the Toy Museum is the German wooden toys, dating from the late-eighteenth through the first decade of the twentieth centuries. The wooden toys include fortresses (fig. 6.1), Noah's arks (fig. 6.3), village blocks (fig. 6.5), train sets (fig. 6.7), and an array of toys created in the mountainous regions of Germany. Of particular interest to scholars, the collection includes three complete, original toy seller's catalogs, and numerous single sheets from other German toy catalogs, all with beautifully hand-colored engraved plates.

Such a large collection of German wooden toys has been assembled for two reasons: First, Germans were the most productive toymakers in the world from the sixteenth century up to the First World War. Second, the Moravians in Salem, North Carolina, regularly ordered toys for their shops, showing allegiance to their father country from whence they immigrated during the mid-eighteenth century.

Salem was not the only American city ordering German toys, and records of advertisements, customs papers, and paintings from the earliest years of the republic indicate that "Nuremberg toys" were constantly available in America. Mary Audrey Apple, a recognized scholar of German toys, wrote an article in the December 2002 issue of *The Magazine Antiques* illustrating the Old Salem Toy Museum collection:

In Nuremberg, craftsmen in wood, glass, clay, and metal were producing children's toys, among other miniature objects, for export, by the end of the sixteenth century. By the eighteenth century the city had earned its reputation as a center of manufacturing and distribution for wooden toys such as the brightly painted dolls, hobbyhorses, trumpets, and dollhouses that were exported to other European countries [and America]. However, Nuremberg merchants were not wholly dependent on local products. The city's location along major north-south and east-west trade routes offered access to far-flung areas of production.

Nuremberg was the recognized toy capital of the world, and German toys continued to be called "Nuremberg wares" throughout the nineteenth century. Centers such as Sonneberg, with their squeak toys, the Erzebirge region, with their ring-cut animals, and the Austrian valley of Gröden (now in Italy), with their chip-carved toys, were the supply sources for such toys.

FIGURE 6.1:
GERMAN CASTLE

Created between 1880 and 1910, this elaborate medieval-style castle is attributed to the firm headed by Ludwig Moritz Gottschalk (1840-1905) of Marienburg, Germany. With numerous turrets, soldiers' quarters, military fortifications, and drawbridges, the castle displays design elements from Gottschalk's "blue" and "red roof" periods.

GPF–4570.1; 4549.3

Wholesalers in towns other than Nuremberg offered their own toy catalogs with hand-colored engraved plates, and today these brilliantly illustrated books are a primary source of information about German toys. The first known to be issued, by Hieronimus Georg Bestelmeier in 1792-93, continued to be published through the 1850s. With over 1,400 individual toys depicted in his *Magazin*, Bestelmeier's catalogs are highly collected today. So, too, are the catalogs of other wholesale firms like Insam and Prinoth (fig. 6.2) of the Grödner Valley in the southern Tyrolian Mountains.

In each town a powerful *verleger* (translated as an agent wholesaler, or middleman) consolidated the wares from families who augmented their modest incomes from farming or mining by producing toys.

Life for these toymaking families became extremely difficult, as they were squeezed by the powerful verlegers, who demanded goods as quickly and cheaply as possible, and the sources of wood became scarce due to forest depletion. These problems subsequently resulted in increasingly inferior products. The families were barely able to maintain a subsistence-level existence. Prices fell so low for the toys that even a whole family, including children, working sixteen hours a day, could not produce enough income to feed themselves.

During the late-nineteenth and early-twentieth centuries, German wood toys fell victim to more inexpensive replacements. Goods in papier-mâché and tinplate slowly overtook demand for handmade wooden toys. And, with the emergence of the American and English toymaking industries in the second half of the nineteenth century, commercially made children's toys were not exclusively imported from Germany.

FIGURE 6.2:
INSAM & PRINOTH
TOY CATALOG

The Toy Museum is fortunate to be able to exhibit one of three known, hand-colored toy catalogs by the toy wholesaler Insam & Prinoth of Grödnerthal, Italy (formerly Austria). Published between 1875 and 1885, the brilliantly illustrated catalog offers marble games, pull toys, jumping jacks, dolls' heads, and a wide variety of hand-made wooden toys fashioned by woodworkers in the mountainous region near Germany. A large watercolor insert in the catalog of a rocking horse has become the logo of the Toy Museum. The catalog is shown here with similar products to those found in the catalog.

GPF–4740.1; 4740.2-45; 4755

FIGURE 6.3:
NOAH'S ARK

Probably the most recognizable toy from nineteenth-century Germany is a Noah's ark. This well-preserved example with its colorful straw veneers was created in the Erzgebirge region, ca. 1870. German toymakers perfected the mass production of small animals by sawing individual profiles of a particular beast from a lathe-turned ring. Other family members would then shape, gesso, and paint the animals before they were shipped to Nuremberg's wholesalers, who compiled complete ark sets for export throughout the world. Perhaps the rarest animals in such a set are the tiny ladybugs or spiders that survived the ever-present threat of young children cutting their teeth on the soft wood.

GPF–4732.1-201

FIGURE 6.4: HUNT SCENE, WITH ORIGINAL BOX

Considered one of the most gracefully designed of all German wooden toys, this hunt scene reminds visitors of a choreographed ballet. Here the gentleman and his dog chase a pack of deer, as well as a wild boar, through the Black Forest. Like the Noah's ark, this hand-painted toy, with its original box, was a product of the Erzgebirge area of Germany, ca. 1840-50.

GPF–5048.1-16

FIGURE 6.5: BOX OF TOWN BLOCKS

Whether cutting animal profiles from a lathe-turned ring or fashioning village blocks, the Erzgebirge region was one of the leading toymaking areas of Germany during the nineteenth century. Oval boxes, similar to this example, could hold farm and hunting scenes, markets, military camps, soldiers, games, or a variety of miniature household objects. Behind the village set, a page from a catalog issued by the Johann Simon Lindner firm of Sonneberg in 1831 depicts similar fortress towns available from this prominent toy wholesaler.

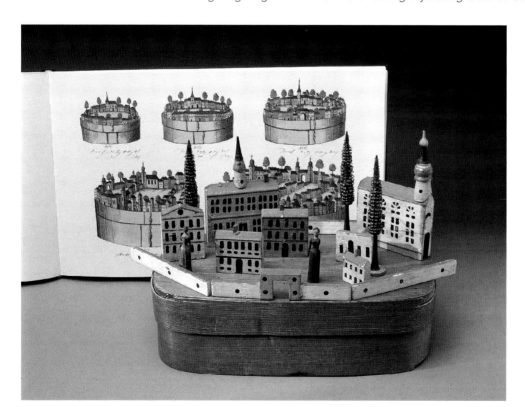

GPF–4567.33

FIGURE 6.6: GROWLING BULLDOG

Though possibly French, this growling bulldog may be from the Sonneberg region of Germany, ca. 1890. A popular artifact for visitors, who hear the growling sounds from the dog during the Toys on the Move video at the museum, the bulldog is a realistic depiction with glass eyes, animal fur, and its original pneumatic device producing a sound more like a slow growl than a bark.

GPF–4669

FIGURE 6.7: WOOD TRAIN SET, WITH ORIGINAL BOX

Certainly one of the most noteworthy German toys in the collection is this train set, with its original box, from the Erzgebirge region, ca. 1850. Plate 39 from the Waldkirchen toy sample book of Carl Heinrich Oehme (1796-1876) depicts an identical toy train. Oehme's father, Georg Carl (1759-1814) founded the firm in 1787, and successive generations gathered toys from home industries in the Erzgebirge Mountain chain and exported the wooden sets through their worldwide trading contacts.

GPF–4592.1; Plate 39, reproduced from *The Toy Sample Book of Waldkirchen: About 1850* by Ruth Michaelis-Jena and Patrick Murray (New York: Hastings House Publishers, 1978). Reproduced with permission of Hastings House/Daytrips Publishers.

CHAPTER 7
TRANSPORTATION TOYS

FOR America, the nineteenth century was a time of dramatic change. Vast economic growth brought mass-production to a nation of factories, and the machine civilization demanded speedier transportation of goods to a country on the verge of world prominence. As Wendell Garrett has written in *Victorian America*:

The faster tempo of this dynamic, freewheeling society revolutionized life in America. Until the Victorian period, the horse and the sailing vessel had set the pace. Now, within a few years, the startling novelty of macadam roads, railroads, improved inland waterways, and ocean-going steamships impressed the Victorians with an intense awareness of speed—a sense of faster and more crowded living. This was a century of insatiable curiosity and restless energy.

While the South was reluctant to abandon its plantation economy and homogeneous rural ways, the North embraced urbanization and industrialization as European immigrants poured into the cities with ambitious abandon. And, with the German newcomers, came advances in all forms of toymaking.

Firefighting equipment, both full scale to protect the emerging cities and toy scale to replicate the splendid adult creations, mirrored the technical advances of the "modernized" nineteenth century. For centuries firefighting had been a volunteer necessity for communities, both urban and rural. The first volunteer fire department was founded by Benjamin Franklin in Philadelphia in 1735, and during the eighteenth and early-nineteenth centuries, hand-drawn equipment and bucket brigades protected people and their possessions. The first manufactured toy fire engines appeared before the Civil War, and about 1880 mass production of tinplate and cast-iron playthings began in earnest (fig. 7.2).

The unique, child-size pumper in fig. 7.1, by Gebrüder Märklin of Göppingen, Germany, represents the advances in tinplate manufacturing. No company took the art of tinplate further than Märklin, which today continues its tradition with exceptional train sets.

The use of tinplate by firms such as Märklin represents one of the greatest inventions in toymaking during the nineteenth century. It was revolutionary because sheets of iron and steel thinly coated with molten tin was inexpensive to make and could easily be mass-produced. Invented in Bohemia

FIGURE 7.1: PUMPER

The "No. 16" child-size pumper is the only known example of this toy by Gebrüder Märklin & Cie, of Göppingen, Germany. Designed to actually shoot water from its rubber hose, the pumper, ca. 1900-02, would have been the envy of many a Victorian child, as today it brings cheers from collectors of this most recognized of all toy manufacturers.

GPF–4502.36

FIGURE 7.2: CAST-IRON FIREFIGHTING TOYS

Two American cast-iron toys, ca. 1890, by the Ives Corporation of Bridgeport, Connecticut, flank "The Fire Engine Puzzle," with its original box, by Peter G. Thomson of Cincinnati, Ohio. Ives is considered one of America's premier toymakers in the later half of the nineteenth century. These examples of horse-drawn, hook-and-ladder and fire patrol wagons exhibit their original paint and cast figures.

GPF–4566.2; 4566.1; 4549.2

(now part of the Czech Republic) around 1620, tin-plating spread throughout Europe and to Britain. Large-scale production in America did not begin until about 1890.

It was the Germans, however, who capitalized on the possibilities of making toys from tinplate. They perfected mass production, adapted their machinery to the new electric power, and wisely used scrap tinplate from other products. Their colorful toys with interchangeable and moving parts set a new standard. The Germans also effectively promoted their toys at trade shows, where they demonstrated how toys were made. Since duty on mechanical toy exports was levied by

weight, the bodies of the toys were made very thin, and thus the appeal for the buyer became the colorful surface decoration—painted, stenciled, or lithographed. The decoration could also be specifically tailored to the countries to which the toys were exported.

If Märklin, founded in 1859, was the premier manufacturer of tinplate trains, then to America goes the honor of developing paper-covered and cast-iron train sets. American toy manufacturers, always on the lookout for ways to reduce labor costs, found that gluing lithographed paper on simple wooden or cardboard shapes could produce an exciting toy, not unlike the wooden

Erzgebirge, Germany, trains described in Chapter 6. Cast-iron trains, like our Wilkins Toy Company example (fig. 7.3), circa 1880, from Keene, New Hampshire, could be inexpensively produced and painted by dipping an entire car in a single color with details added by using a rubber stamp. The first of the established American companies to manufacture cast-iron trains was Ives of Plymouth, Connecticut, which was producing trackless, hand-operated and clockwork locomotives and trains by the 1880s, listing them in its catalogs alongside antiquated tin locomotives.

The durable, cast-iron floor trains of America replicated the immense, cross-

country trains that linked the four corners of a country restless for mobility and migration. As the nineteenth century drew to a close, horse-drawn vehicles (figs. 7.4 and 7.5) were replaced by horseless carriages, and remote populations evolved into commuting suburbs.

Just as the company founded by Theodore Fredrich Märklin (1817-66) moved from producing kitchenware for dollhouses in the 1870s to trains and ships in the 1880s to cars after 1900, other leading tinplate designers also quickly adapted to the changing market, reproducing cars like the American curved-dash Oldsmobile in 1903 (fig. 7.6).

The full-sized, curved-dash Oldsmobile automobile stands as America's first mass-produced car, emerging in 1900 with a price tag of $650. In 1905, the Acme Toy Works of Chicago, Illinois, produced two patented, clockwork toys: the curved-dash Oldsmobile and a delivery truck, both in pressed steel. Despite a time lag of three years between the full-sized automobile and the toy replica, the toys were popular amusements for American children until the Acme Toy Works were dissolved in 1908.

Two additional transportation modes are also widely represented in the Toy Museum: boats—including pleasure and military examples—and the earliest airplane, with its origins on North Carolina's Outer Banks.

Two naval vessels—the ironclad *Monitor* (fig. 7.7) from the Civil War period, and the battleship *New York* (fig. 7.8) from the Spanish-American War—can be used to show the differences in time, design, and finish between an American and a German toy-making firm.

The tinplate *Monitor* toy, and the accompanying watercolor sketch by its creator, George Brown of Forrestville, Connecticut, stand out among the jewels of our collection.

FIGURE 7.4: HORSE-DRAWN SURRY

This example is the only known surry of its type by Althof, Bergmann & Company of New York City. Created ca. 1875, the tinplate carriage was propelled by a key-wound clockwork mechanism, and the porcelain-headed lady passenger appears quite happy being driven through a make-believe park. Althof, Bergmann & Company began production in the 1860s and is known for its elaborate, hand-painted tin toys,

GPF–4733.3

One of only three known examples, the vessel by Brown, circa 1862-72, reflects the honest integrity of solid yet simple design particular to American toys of the early Victorian period. In contrast, the battleship *New York*, circa 1900, by Märklin, is as elaborately detailed and accessorized as any naval boat to be created at the end of the Victorian era. Märklin's pre-eminence in tinplate toymaking is evident throughout this hand-painted example.

No chapter on transportation would be complete without the introduction of flight, the ultimate feat accomplished by man. The ability to fly linked not only continents, but also expanded worldwide imaginations. The accomplishments of the Wright brothers on December 17, 1903, at Kitty Hawk, North Carolina, were a virtual Christmas present to humankind. Children accustomed to immediate reproductions of "adult con-

traptions," quickly received gifts of biplane replicas (fig. 7.9), finely detailed and ready for imagined flights to places unknown. The era of discovery and transportation had truly entered a "magical" time.

FIGURE 7.5: HORSE-DRAWN STREET CAR

The "Broadway—Main Street—City Hall" horse-drawn streetcar is attributed to Ludwig Moritz Gottschalk (1840-1905), of Marienberg, Germany. Complete with its original horses covered with actual horsehide, this handsome streetcar with New York City destinations was obviously intended for the late-nineteenth-century American market. A driver doll by Simon & Halbig of Thuringia, Germany, with his original uniform and whip, dates from the same period.

GPF–4499.1; 4502.2

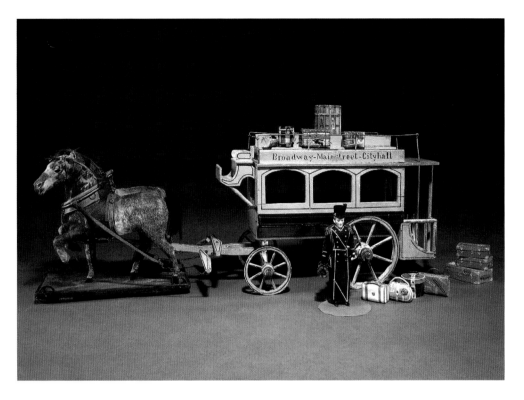

FIGURE 7.6: EARLY AUTOMOBILES

Children's toys throughout history directly reflected the most recent technological advances of the adult world. So it was with the introduction of the "horseless carriage" in the late-nineteenth century. Clockwise from the bottom left are a touring car with the original canvas top by Hans Eberl, ca. 1910, from Nuremberg, Germany; a second, red, touring car, ca. 1908, by Morton E. Converse Company of Winchendon, Massachusetts; a limousine, ca. 1911, by Georges Carette & Cie of Nuremberg; a curved-dash Oldsmobile, ca. 1903, by the Acme Toy Works of Chicago, Illinois; and a vis-á-vis car, ca. 1898, by Gunthermann of Nuremberg.

GPF–4680; 4502.16; 4638; 4503.8; 4737.1

FIGURE 7.7: *MONITOR,* WITH ORIGINAL WATERCOLOR

The Monitor clockwork boat and accompanying watercolor must be considered two of the highlights of the Toy Museum. Created by George W. Brown of Forrestville, Connecticut, between 1862 and 1872,

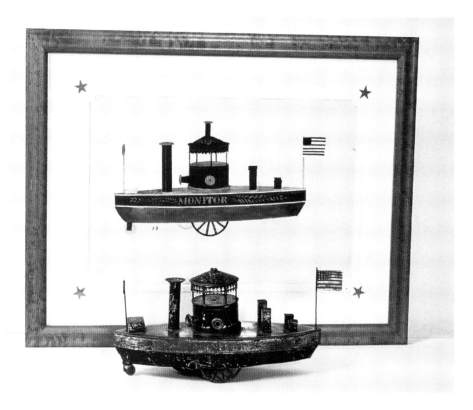

the ship was propelled by a clockwork mechanism. The watercolor, drawn by Brown to scale, was both a working sketch for production purposes and a pattern for an entry for his trade catalog. This tinplate toy, replicating the famous Civil War ironclad, is especially relevant today as the actual Monitor was discovered by marine archaeologists in 1973 off the coast of Cape Hatteras, North Carolina. The ironclad sank on December 30, 1862, while being towed to port for repairs.

GPF–4733.1

FIGURE 7.8: *NEW YORK* BATTLESHIP

The USS New York was launched in 1891 and commissioned in 1893. This toy representation of the famous ship, ca. 1900, is a fine example of history influencing the toy industry, as well

as Märklin's predominance in toy shipbuilding. The New York was the flagship of the combined "North American Squadron" and the "Flying Squadron" commanded by Admiral Sampson during the Spanish-American War, and she played a major part in the Battle of Santiago. During this war, the New York is credited with actions against eleven Spanish vessels and, because of her notoriety, was received with great celebration when she sailed into New York harbor on August 14, 1898.

GPF–4702.1

FIGURE 7.9: EARLY AIRPLANES

On December 17, 1903, at Kitty Hawk, North Carolina, Wilbur and Orville Wright, two bicycle mechanics from Dayton, Ohio, achieved what few men had only dreamed of—the first successful flight. Toymakers, especially in Germany, responded to the breaking news with their own interpretations of the famous "flying machine." On the right, a tinplate biplane by H. Fisher & Co., ca. 1910, of Nuremberg, is complemented by a biplane swing fairground ride on the left by Müller & Kadeder, ca. 1905-08, also of Nuremberg. The tiny biplanes in the foreground were Christmas ornaments from Dresden, Germany, about 1905.

GPF–4736.1; 4767.1: 4180.7; 4865.1

CHAPTER 8
CHILDREN'S SPORTS EQUIPMENT

The Old Salem Toy Museum displays a collection of youth sports equipment unlike that found in any other toy museum in America. In addition to baseball and football items, tennis, golf, and basketball are also represented by uniforms, board games, early leather balls, and children's trophies.

During the eighteenth century in North Carolina, horseracing, cockfighting, fishing, hunting, and "gouging" (a particularly gruesome sport combining boxing, wrestling, and maiming) were the predominant sporting activities. Not until the post-Civil War period did one see the introduction of football, baseball, golf, and tennis—all enjoyed both by children and adults in this "sport state."

Even in the seventeenth century, John Amos Comenius recognized the importance of exercise for children:

Children must also have daily exercises and excitements. It was first for this purpose that people developed the custom of rocking babies in cradles...or pulling them in wagons...when babies grow up a little, however, and begin to take to their feet, they should be allowed to run.... The more a child is active, runs about, and plays, the sweeter is its sleep, the more easily does its stomach digest, the more quickly does it grow and flourish both in body and mind.

Although formally organized in the northeast, the game of baseball evolved from a number of children's bat-and-ball games. In 1862 during the Civil War, prisoners of war detained in Salisbury, North Carolina, were recorded playing baseball. By the conclusion of the war, a number of modern rules for baseball were in place, including the nine-man team, the three-out inning, and the nine-inning game. Fig. 8.1 shows a child's uniform and accoutrements for baseball, ca. 1890-1900.

Fig. 8.2 shows the football equipment needed to properly outfit a child about 1900. Football was largely associated with college students until well into the twentieth century. The earliest games, traced to 1869, closely resembled soccer, in which ball advances could only be accomplished by kicking or heading. An 1874 Harvard-McGill match first allowed advancement of the ball by running.

Americans today understand the game of football as two eleven-member teams, each of whose purpose is to carry, or pass and catch, an ovoid ball across the opponent's goal line. Outside the United States, however, "football" can describe a number of games, including rugby, soccer, or Australian football. Soccer is an abbreviation for "Association Football," established in the United Kingdom about 1890-95. Rugby is a version called "Rugby Football," established at the boys school of the same name in East Warwickshire, England.

FIGURE 8.1: BASEBALL EQUIPMENT

Long considered the American national pastime, baseball is today a popular sport for children of all ages. On the mannequin, the child's "Peacock" uniform by Sporting Goods Manufacturing Co. of New York, ca. 1900, is displayed with a "Junior Nine" straw cap and a ringed bat by Spaulding of New Hampshire, both of the same period. The small figure of a baseball player is actually a candy container from the Sonneberg area of Germany, ca. 1880. The board game, "The Champion Game of Baseball," was manufactured by Proctor Amusement Co. of North Cambridge, Massachusetts, ca. 1890.

GPF–4637.2; 4670.11; 4582.2; 4577.1; 4682.2; 4581.2; 4667.3; 4637.1

FIGURE 8.2: FOOTBALL EQUIPMENT

Despite occasional broken limbs and bloody noses, football has long been a favorite sport for young children. The mannequin displays a leather child's helmet by Wilson Sporting Goods Co., cotton pants and shoes by unknown American makers, and a youth football by an unknown American manufacturer, all ca. 1900-10. The papier-mâché football player candy container from the Sonneberg area of Germany, ca. 1905, is shown with one of the many early children's sports novels in the museum's collection.

GPF–4684.1; 4582.1; 4760.2; 5083; 4667.7; 4667.6; 4586.1; 4574

CHAPTER 9
SEASONAL TOYS

A wonderful array of toys and decorations for every season of the year awaits visitors to the Toy Museum, and in the changing exhibit area of the museum holiday toys rotate throughout the year with the seasons they represent.

The great majority of seasonal toys and decorations were fabricated in Germany. Technological advancements there propelled Germany to lead the world in exporting lithographed, papered, and veneered products until the start of World War I.

From mid-February, early St. Valentine's Day cards by the leading designers in America, England, and Germany reflect the Victorian love of hand-colored images, as well as lace, foldout, and honeycombed designs. George Washington's birthday (fig. 9.1) on February 22 was celebrated at the turn of the twentieth century with candy containers designed to look like the general astride his horse, or like his infamous cherry tree complete with buried hatchet.

The Christian holiday of Easter commemorates Christ's rising from the dead, as well as the ancient springtime festivals of nature coming back to life. The spring holiday of new life is represented by newborn animals, especially lambs, rabbits, and chickens, which German firms in the Sonneberg area molded in papier-mâché as candy containers and Easter eggs (fig. 9.2).

After America's patriotic July Fourth and summer vacations, the fall season awaits Halloween on October 31. Historically the day, also called All Hallows' Eve, was a holy or hallowed evening observed on the last day of October, the eve of All Saints' Day. It was also based on an ancient pagan Celtic lore surrounding harvest and seasonal changes, coinciding with the date when dead souls were to revisit their homes. Thus, this autumnal festival acquired fiendish significance, with the thoughts of ghosts, witches, and demons roaming about. Primarily designed for the American market between 1900-20, the German pumpkin lanterns and witch candy containers (fig. 9.3) were eagerly purchased by late-Victorian youngsters.

Following a full bounty on Thanksgiving, the Christmas season is the most significant celebration of the calendar year. Christmas! The very word excites children as much as their parents revere this special season. Christmas has been celebrated on December 25 since the fourth century, a date

FIGURE 9.1: GEORGE WASHINGTON'S BIRTHDAY

Today we acknowledge the legacy of our first president, General George Washington (1732-99), by remembering his birthday on February 22. A congressional resolution in 1799 instituted February 22, 1800, as a day to honor America's founding father. Here, two candy containers from the Sonneberg area of Germany, ca. 1900-10, represent toys and decorations available for children to recognize this historic occasion.

GPF–4978; 5022

FIGURE 9.2: EASTER TOYS

Virtually every seasonal decoration and toy from the late-nineteenth and early-twentieth centuries originated in Germany. This sample group of Easter toys was manufactured in the Sonneberg area of Germany, ca. 1880-1910. From a papier-mâché egg, filled with Little Bo Peep and her sheep, to a fine rabbit candy container being ridden by a bisque-head doll, the toys for this spring season in the museum's collection are endless in their magic and variety.

GPF–4500.1; 4670.7

FIGURES 9.3a AND 9.3b: HALLOWEEN TOYS

The mere mention of the holiday's name, "Halloween," elicits images of sinister ghosts, witches, and jack-ó-lanterns. In the early-twentieth century, German manufacturers vividly created toys— primarily lanterns and candy containers—for the occasion from their shops in the Sonneberg area. The wood nutcracker above on the left is a particularly rare toy with vegetable-shaped body parts, and the Halloween crepe paper shown below is especially graphic and colorful.

GPF–4965; 4931; 4899.1; 4901.1; 4901.2; 5102.4 (crepe paper)

chosen not for religious reasons, but because it was close to the winter solstice, an established pre-Christian festival. The season was often welcomed by rowdy public revelry, a tradition that continued into the nineteenth century in Europe, Britain, and America.

In addition to merrymaking, gift giving was observed, and there were many newspaper advertisements listing suitable "Christmas presents." One advertisement from Baltimore in 1809 offered:

a large assortment of all kinds of toys, German and English, and all sorts of SUGARS, Christmas CAKES, also, PASTRY… . Parents who wish to please their children, during the holidays, are invited to call and view the shop.

By the last quarter of the nineteenth century, more people had more money and time to invest in Christmas celebrations. "Feather trees," favored in Germany because of their small size and to encourage tree conservation, were exported throughout the world and available to Victorian families in all sizes. Bird feathers, dyed green, were wrapped together with wire and then inserted as branches into a paper-wrapped wooden trunk. Gold-and silver-foiled cardboard ornaments stamped out in Dresden, Germany, decorated these unusual trees, and candles, actually lighted after being placed in counter-weighted holders, produced a truly magical sight.

German craftsmen also fabricated Father Christmas and Santa Claus figures as two-part-body candy containers (fig. 9.4). Santa Claus, one of the most widespread and best-loved symbols of Christmas, was based on the story of St. Nicholas, Bishop of Myra, who, in the fourth century, became a legend in his lifetime for his benevolence. His good works conveyed the goodness that Christ's life and message taught, and the figures were blended over the centuries into one manifestation of sharing with others. Dr. Clement Moore, with his "Visit from St. Nicholas" in 1822, firmly established the modern Christmas legend.

FIGURE 9.4: CHRISTMAS TOYS

More than any other season, Christmas became, during the Victorian period, a festive time for extraordinary decorations and gifts. From candy containers molded as Father Christmas to Santa figures pulled by reindeer in a moss sleigh, German designs in the Sonneberg area between 1880 and 1900 met every imaginable desire of young worshipers and revelers.

GPF–4578.26; 4578.25; 4561 (Belsnickel candy container), in memory of Dr. George E. Waynick Jr.; 4500.2; 4899.10; 4865.4

SELECTED BIBLIOGRAPHY

Evelyn Ackerman, *Dolls in Miniature: A Portrayal of Society Through Tiny Dolls, Their Fashions, and Environments, 1700-1930* (Annapolis, MD: Gold Horse Publishing, 1991).

_____, *The Genius of Moritz Gottschalk: Blue and Red Roof Dollhouses, Stores, Kitchens, Stables, and Other Miniature Structures* (Annapolis, MD: Gold Horse Publishing, 1994).

_____, *Under the Bigtop with Schoenhut's Humpty Dumpty Circus* (Annapolis, MD: Gold Horse Publishing, 1996).

Carlernst Baecker, Dieter Haas, and Claude Jean Marie, Märklin, *From the Founding to the Turn of the Century, 1859-1902* (New York: Hastings House Publishers, 1978).

Carlernst Baecker and Christian Väterlein, *Germany's Forgotten Toymakers* (Frankfurt, Germany: Verlag der Frankfurter Fachbuchhandlung Michael Kohl, 1982).

Christian Bailly, *Automata, The Golden Age, 1848-1914* (London: Sotheby's Publications, 1987).

Richard Balzer, *Peepshows: A Visual History* (New York: Harry N. Abrams, 1998).

Bernard Barenholtz and Inez McClintock, *American Antique Toys, 1830-1900* (New York: Harry N. Abrams, 1998).

Edith F. Barenholtz, ed., *The George Brown Toy Sketchbook* (Princeton, NJ: Pyre Press, 1971).

R.C. Bell, *The Boardgame Book* (Los Angeles: Knapp Press, 1979).

Stanley A. Block, *Marble Mania* (Atglen, PA: Schiffer Publishing, 1998).

Patricia Brady, ed., *George Washington's Beautiful Nelly* (Columbia: University of South Carolina Press, 1991).

Robert Brenner, *Christmas Through the Decades* (Atglen, PA: Schiffer Publishing, 1993).

Dr. R. Alexander Briggs, *Coral, Whistles, and Bells* (Appleby, England: The Millennium, 1999).

Olivia Bristol and Leslie Geddes-Brown, *Dolls' Houses: Domestic Life and Architectural Styles in Miniature from the Seventeenth Century to the Present Day* (London: Mitchell Beazley, 1997).

George Buday, *The History of the Christmas Card* (London: Spring Books, 1954).

Jürgen Cieslik and Marianne Cieslik, *Button in Ear, The History of the Teddy Bear and His Friends* (Jülich, West Germany: Marianne Cieslik Verlag, 1989).

_____, *Teddy Bear Encyclopedia* (Jülich, West Germany: Marianne Cieslik Verlag, 1998).

Dorothy S. Coleman, Elizabeth A. Coleman, and Evelyn J. Coleman, *The Collector's Encyclopedia of Dolls* (New York: Crown Publishers, 1989).

Al Davidson, Penny Lane, *A History of Antique Mechanical Banks* (Mokelumne Hill, CA: Long's Americana, 1987).

Judith Anderson Drawe and Kathleen Bridge Greenstein, *Lithographed Paper Toys, Books, and Games* (Atglen, PA: Schiffer Publishing, 2000).

Geoff Egan, *Playthings from the Past, Toys from the A.G. Pilson Collection, c.1300-1800* (London: Jonathan Horne Publications, 1996).

Stephanie Finnegan, *The Dollhouse Book* (New York: Black Dog and Lerenthal Publishers, 1999).

Hazel Forsyth and Geoff Egan, *Toys, Trifles, & Trinkets: Base-Metal Miniatures from London, 1200 to 1800* (London: Museum of London, 2005).

Jan Foulke, Simon & Halbig *Dolls, The Artful Aspect* (Cumberland, MD: Hobby Horse Press, 1984).

Antonia Fraser, *A History of Toys* (New York: Spring Books, 1972).

Wendell Garrett, *Victoria America: Classical Romanticism to Gilded Opulence* (New York: Rizzoli, 1993).

Pier Giorgio and Luca Gracis, *Miniature English Furniture* (Milan, Italy: Pier Giorgio and Luca Gracis, 2000).

Lillian Gottschalk, *American Motortoys, 1894-1942* (London: New Cavendish Books, 1986).

Christine Gräfnitz, *German Papier-Mâché Dolls, 1760-1860* (Duisburg, Germany: Verlag Puppen & Spielzarg, 1994).

Peter Haining, *Movable Books: An Illustrated History* (London: New English Library, 1979).

Charles V. Hansen, *The History of American Firefighting Toys* (Sykesville, MD: Greenburg Publishing, 1990).

Mary Hillier, *Automata and Mechanical Toys* (London: Jupiter, 1976).

Morton A. Hirschberg, *Steam Toys: A Symphony in Motion* (Atglen, PA: Schiffer Publishing, 1996).

Dr. Chris Holloway and Felicity Marno, *Caughley Porcelain Toy Wares* (London: Dr. Chris Holloway and Felicity Marno, 2001).

Victor Houart, *Miniature Silver Toys* (New York: Alpine Fine Arts Collection, 1981).

Bernard Hughes and Therle Hughes, *Collecting Miniature Antiques* (London: Heinemann, 1973).

Flora Gill Jacobs, *Dolls' Houses in America: Historic Preservation in Miniature* (New York: Charles Scribner's Sons, 1974).

Constance Eileen King, *Christmas Antiques, Decorations, and Traditions* (Woodbridge, England: Antique Collectors' Club, 1999).

_____, *The Collector's History of Dolls' Houses, Doll's House Dolls, and Miniatures* (New York: St. Martin's Press, 1983).

_____, *The Encyclopedia of Toys* (New York: Crown Publishers, 1978).

Karl Ewald Kritzch and Manfred Bachmann, *An Illustrated History of German Toys* (New York: Hastings House Publishers, 1978).

Henry I. Kurtz and Burtt R. Ehrlich, *The Art of the Toy Soldier* (New York: Abbeville Press, 1987).

Ruth Webb Lee, *A History of Valentines* (Wellesley Hills, MA: Lee Publishers, 1952).

Tim Luke, *Toys from American Childhood* (Cumberland, MD: Portfolio Press, 2001).

Katherine Morrison McClinton, *Antiques in Miniature* (New York: Charles Scribner's Sons, 1970).

_____, *Antiques of American Childhood* (New York: Bramshall House, 1970).

Maurice Milbourn and Evelyn Milbourn, *Understanding Miniature British Pottery and Porcelain, 1730 – Present Day* (London: Antique Collectors' Club, 1983).

Jacques Milet and Robert Forbes, *Toy Boats, 1870-1955: A Pictorial History* (New York: Charles Scribner's Sons, 1979).

Patricia Mullins, *The Rocking Horse: A History of Moving Toy Horses* (London: New Cavendish Books, 1992).

Bill Norman, *The Encyclopedia of Mechanical Bank Collecting* (San Diego, CA: Accent Studios, 1985).

Richard O'Brien, *The Story of American Toys, from the Puritans to the Present* (London: New Cavendish Books, 1990).

James Opie, *The Great Book of Britans, 100 Years of Britans Toy Soldiers, 1893-1993* (London: New Cavendish Books, 1993).

Jet Pijzel-Dommisse, *Het Hollandse Pronkpoppenhuis, Interieur en Huishouden in de 17de. En 18de. eeuw* (Amsterdam: Rijksmuseum, n.d.).

David Pressland, *The Art of the Tin Toy* (London: New Cavendish Books, 1976).

_____, *The Book of Penny Toys* (London: New Cavendish Books, 1991).

Rick Ralston, *Cast Iron Floor Trains, an Encyclopedia with Rarity and Price Guide* (Aiea, HI: Ralston Publishing, 1994).

Jac Remise and Jean Fondin, *The Golden Age of Toys* (Lausanne, Switzerland: Edita S.A. Lausanne, 1967).

Sally Revill-Davies, *Yesterday's Children: The Antiques and History of Childcare* (Woodbridge, England: Antique Collectors' Club, 1991).

David L. Ribblett, *Nelly Custis, Child of Mount Vernon* (Mount Vernon, VA: Mount Vernon Ladies' Association, 1993).

Hans Henning Roer, *Old German Toy Soldiers* (Rommersheim, Germany: Palagonia Verlag, 1993).

Edward Ryan, Paper Soldiers, *The Illustrated History of Printed Paper Armies of the 18th, 19th, and 20th Centuries* (London: Golden Age Editions, 1995).

Herbert F. Schiffer and Peter B. Schiffer, *Miniature Antique Furniture, Doll House and Children's Furniture from the United States and Europe* (Atglen, PA: Schiffer Publishing, 1995).

Margaret Schiffer, *Holidays, Toys and Decorations* (West Chester, PA: Schiffer Publishing, 1985).

Paul Klein Schiphorst, *The Golden Years of Tin Toy Trains, 1850-1909* (London: New Cavendish Books, 2002).

Stuart Schneider, *Halloween in America* (Atglen, PA: Schiffer Publishing, 1995).

Simon Spero, *The Simpson Collection of Eighteenth Century English Blue and White Miniature Porcelain* (London: Simon Spero, 2003).

Rita Stäblein and Robert Moroder, *La Vedla Chiena de Gherdëina* (St. Ulrich, Italy: Museum de Gherdëina, 1994).

James Christen Steward, *The New Child: British Art and the Origins of Modern Childhood 1730-1830* (Berkeley: University of California, 1995).

Jane Toller, *Antique Miniature Furniture in Great Britain and America* (London: G. Bell & Sons, 1966).

Margaret Towner, *Doll's House Furniture* (London: Apple Press, 1993).

F.R.B. Whitehouse, *Table Games of Georgian and Victorian Days* (Royston, England: Priory Press, 1971).

Blair Whitton, *American Clockwork Toys, 1862-1900* (Exton, PA: Schiffer Publishing, 1981).

_____, *Paper Toys of the World* (Cumberland, MD: Hobby Horse Press, 1986).

Peter Williams and Pat Halfpenny, *A Passion of Pottery: Further Selections from the Henry H. Weldon Collection* (New York: Sotheby's Publications, 2000).